VGM Opportunities Series

OPPORTUNITIES IN COUNSELING AND DEVELOPMENT CAREERS

Neale J. Baxter

Foreword by
Patrick J. McDonough, Ed. D., NCC
Executive Director
American Association for Counseling and Development

Careers
1211 10th St. SW   Box 135
LARGO, FL 34649-0135
(813) 584-7333

Cover Photo Credits:
Front cover: upper left and lower right, Charter Medical Corporation photos; upper right, NTC photo; lower left, photo courtesy of Neale Baxter.
Back cover: upper and lower left, Charter Medical Corporation photos; upper right, photo by Bill Styles; lower right, Council of International Programs photo.

Library of Congress Cataloging-in-Publication Data

Baxter, Neale.
    Opportunities in counseling and development careers / Neale J. Baxter.
        p. cm. — (VGM opportunities series)
    Bibliography: p.
    ISBN 0-8442-8656-7 : $11.95. — ISBN 0-8442-8657-5 (soft) : $8.95
    1. Counseling—Vocational guidance. I. Title. II. Series.
BF637.C6B285   1989
361.3′23′02373--dc20   89-14795
                                                                             CIP

Published by VGM Career Horizons, a division of NTC Publishing Group.
© 1990 by NTC Publishing Group, 4255 West Touhy Avenue,
Lincolnwood (Chicago), Illinois 60646-1975 U.S.A.
All rights reserved. No part of this book may be reproduced, stored in a retrieval system, or transmitted in any form or by any means, electronic, mechanical, photocopying, recording or otherwise, without the prior permission of NTC Publishing Group.
Manufactured in the United States of America.

9 0 VP 9 8 7 6 5 4 3 2 1

ABOUT THE AUTHOR

Neale Baxter has published widely on a great variety of occupations, including two previous VGM books, *Opportunities in Federal Government Careers* and *Opportunities in State and Local Government Careers*. His award-winning articles have appeared in such diverse publications as *The Occupational Outlook Quarterly, The Monthly Labor Review, Career World,* and the Washington *Post.* He is currently the managing editor of a magazine published by the federal government. He earned a bachelor's degree from Manhattan College, a master's from Purdue University, and a Ph.D. from the University of North Carolina at Chapel Hill. He lives in Virginia with his wife Anne and his children, Kathleen and Tom.

ACKNOWLEDGMENTS

Thanks are due, as always, to Kathleen, Tom, and Anne, who provide a reason to work on books like this and welcome respites from working on them.

Many people generously shared their experience and knowledge with me, thus making this book possible. The twenty-two experts quoted in chapter 19 must be mentioned first: Olie Ahlquist, Les Blankenship, William A. Bryan, Jon Dalton, Tom Gertz, Ken Hoyt, Dorothy Jenkins, John Keyser, Richard LaFon, Dennis Martin, Carl McDaniels, Frederick E. Menz, Fred Otte, Duane Parker, Bill Richardson, Dorothy Thomas, Jean A. Thompson, Edwin A. Whitfield, Richard R. Wilmarth, Gaynelle Wilson, Jim Wilson, and George Wright. In addition to the statements attributed to them there, they provided me with hundreds of leads and innumerable pieces of information that have been quietly incorporated into the text.

Among the many other counselors, researchers, and association professionals who were also helpful are the following: Bill Abbot, Jim Banning, Carol Bonnie, Douglas Brown, Frank Burtnett, Mike Chrin, Dan Crowe, Sandra Dennis, Jack Donohue, Bertie Firestone, Wilton Fowler, Janet Fumanti, Jan Gelardo, Daniel Hecker, Barbara Huffman, Thuman Huynh, Gayla Keese, Joanne Kipnis, Steve Krammer, Dannielle LeMolle, Tom Leif, Frank Lisnoou, Paul Lubben, Susan Mason, Joe Maxwell, Madelin McClean, Elizabeth McGregor, Kay Monks, Ludmilla Murphy, Rhea Nagle, Carol Neiman, Helen Paton, Bill Pierce, Georgine Pion, JoAnn Puerling, Bonnie Raines, Jim Reed, T.F. Rigger, Lynn Slavenski, Mary

Stanley, Charles L. Thompson, Steven Townsend, Nancy Whelan, Viki Wildermuth, Michael Witkin, Ray Woodruff, and, especially, Sylvia Nissenoff, who pointed me in new directions more than once when I encountered a dead end.

Some books that were helpful to me are listed in appendix B. Mention should be made here, however, of authors and speakers whose works were especially informative: F. Stephen Alexander, Richard Bolles, Richard W. Daniel, Thomas K. Fagan, Norman C. Gysbers, Joseph W. Hollis, J. Anthony Humphreys, Earl J. More, Donald Mortensen, Robert D. North, Elizabeth Ogg, John J. Pietrofesa, Daniel Robinson, Alan Schmuller, Bruce Shertzer, Michael Stanton, Joy Stapp, Shelley C. Stone, E.L. Tolbert, Arthur E. Traxler, Richard A. Wantz, William J. Weikel, and C. Gilbert Wrenn.

Special thanks are due to five counselors who took time from their busy schedules to discuss their work in detail: Mary Ashton, Fred Hechlinger, Ellissia Price, Linda Seligman, and Francis A. Thomas. The chapters on the nature of the work for different kinds of counselors are based on their comments, although some adjustments were made both to protect the privacy of their clients and to fit the format of this work. Despite their assistance, some errors may have crept into these or other chapters; in such cases the fault is entirely my own.

FOREWORD

The exciting thing about the content and new material you are about to look at, read, and page through in this book is its freshness! Career books abound. And there are even some other books which describe careers in the field of counseling and human development. But nowhere has anyone talked about the contribution that counseling and human development make to the enhancement of the human condition in such a definitive way. This book tries!

Counseling is as old as the history of the human race. Mohammed (using the Koran as his text), Moses (and the Bible), Jesus (and the Old and New Testaments), Buddha, and others have given advice down through the years and have tried to help people in bettering their lives and solving their problems.

However, the practice of counseling and human development as currently conceived is unique, because now a systematically prepared group of professionally trained people are available to deal with the normal range of problems that people experience. This group of professionals we call counselors and human development specialists. The author of this book has made a special effort to give a historical perspective to the growth of the counseling and human development movement in the United States. He describes the various aspects of counseling and the theories that underlie the practice of counseling in its many forms and its various settings. Counselors and human development specialists are clearly separated from other mental health professionals like psychologists and psychiatrists. So, students like yourself in high school settings can get a clear picture of what counselors do and how one could be prepared to become a counselor.

Therefore, you will be able to make better career choice decisions if you are, in fact, interested in the counseling and human development field as a choice for your life work. I would urge each of you reading this book to work closely with your school counselor or career development specialist in the career exploration process. In exploring careers in the counseling and human development field your challenge will be, where do I fit? How do I prepare? Where do I get trained if I want to be a counselor or human development specialist? *Opportunities in Counseling and Development Careers* will be a major assistance to you in answering those questions in this particular professional field.

Such are the exciting decisions that you will be facing as you explore the world of work!

When one looks at America, its strengths and its weaknesses, it is apparent that where it needs help is in its humanizing aspect. The new and exciting field of counseling and human development is a "clam shell" opening, offering many potential opportunities in careers dedicated to enhancing the human condition. The following pages will be a major help in your determination of whether a career in this mental health field is an appropriate choice for you.

> Patrick J. McDonough, Ed. D., NCC
> Executive Director
> American Association for Counseling
> and Development

CONTENTS

About the Author iii
Acknowledgments iv
Foreword vi
1. **Prelude: Counseling, a Caring Profession** 1
2. **The Varieties of Counseling** 5
   Types of counselors. Functions of counselors. Counseling services and settings.
3. **High School Counselors: Squeezing a Year into Ten Months** 11
4. **Elementary School Counselors: What a Day!** 15
5. **Rehabilitation: From Assessment to Employment** 19
6. **Mental Health Counselors in Private Practice: An Interview** 23
7. **School Counselors: Facts and Figures** 27
   Other job titles. Goals and duties. Secondary school counselors. Elementary school counselors. Middle and junior high school counselors. Employment and outlook. Salary, other benefits, and working conditions. Entry

requirements and career ladder. A note on independent educational consultants.

8. **Mental Health Counselors: Facts and Figures** 39

Other job titles. Goals and duties. Employment and outlook. Salary, other benefits, and working conditions. Entry requirements and career ladder.

9. **Rehabilitation Counselors: Facts and Figures** 43

Other job titles. Goals and duties. Employment and outlook. Salary, other benefits, and working conditions. Entry requirements and career ladder.

10. **College Counselors and Student Affairs Administrators: Facts and Figures** 49

Other job titles. Goals and duties. Employment and outlook. Salary, other benefits, and working conditions. Entry requirements and career ladder.

11. **Employment and Career Counselors: Facts and Figures** 57

Other job titles. Goals and duties. Employment and outlook. Salary, other benefits, and working conditions. Entry requirements and career ladder.

12. **Other Counseling and Counseling-Related Occupations** 63

Alcohol and drug abuse counselor. Counseling psychologist. Counselor educator. Member of the clergy. Paraprofessional. Psychiatrist. Pupil personnel worker. School psychologist. Social worker.

13. **Characteristics of a Counselor** 77

What makes a good counselor? Downers and uppers.

Contents xi

14. Education for Counselors 81
Picking a program. What do you learn? What is it like? Trends to keep track of.

15. Counseling's Past 89
Early programs. Progress in counseling.

16. Counseling's Present: Approaches and Techniques ... 93
Current approaches to counseling. Interviewing and group counseling.

17. Current Issues in Counseling 97
Third-party payment. Licensure and certification. Counseling, psychiatry, and psychology. The counselor's role.

18. Counseling's Future 103
Computerized counseling. More work with adults. Counselors in new settings: private sector, private practice.

19. Advice from the Experts 107

20. Coda: Counseling, a Healing Profession 113

Appendix A: National Associations and Certification Authorities 115

Appendix B: Books about College, Graduate School, Careers, and Counseling 125

Appendix C: State Accrediting and Licensing Authorities .. 129

Counselors search for ways to show people how to deal with problems. This rehabilitation counselor is helping a client with a spinal cord injury develop work skills. (photo courtesy of the Rehabilitation Institute of Chicago)

CHAPTER 1

PRELUDE: COUNSELING, A CARING PROFESSION

Caring means listening when you would rather be talking.
—Anonymous student, quoted by C. Gilbert Wrenn

Counseling is a caring profession—know that from the start. Counselors do not seek great economic rewards. They do not search for high adventure. They do not hope to control corporations or crave to be a weekly item in *People* magazine.

Counselors care about other people. They seek methods to help people help themselves. They search for ways to show people how to deal with problems. They hope to put people in charge of themselves.

A definition is in order. Often, the hardest words to define are those we think we know best. We easily describe the connections between people as a *network,* but our definition of *net* is likely to become more obscure the harder we try to clarify it. Dr. Johnson, who wrote a famous dictionary in the eighteenth century, defined *net* as "Anything made with interstitial vacuities." He might better have written, "Go ask a fisherman to show you one." Counseling might be even harder to define; after all, even when you look at a counselor, you won't see counseling.

Here is one possible definition: counseling is working with other people to increase their understanding of themselves, their goals, and their options so that their future behavior can lead them to those goals. This definition would be fine except that it is both too broad (parents and travel agents could fit in it) and too vague (you could increase someone's self-understanding by painting a portrait or giving a lecture).

The definition is correct, however, in the stress it puts on the person the counselor works with.

Counselors recognize the dignity of the individual and the differences among people; they accept the freedom of individuals to set their own goals. Dr. Edwin L. Herr brought out this point in testimony before the U.S. Senate. He said,

> Guidance and counseling in some countries are little more than selection and classification processes devised to separate citizens into areas which serve the national interest. Guidance and counseling in the United States, at least in its philosophical tenets, has derived from a different tradition. Here the emphasis is primarily upon the individual's capability to direct him or herself in the light of social and moral values defined within a belief system that opportunity exists, that challenge confronts him or her, that personal effort will have personal meaning.

The definition is also correct in its emphasis on future behavior, for the purpose of counseling is to change behavior or bring about a reorientation of the client's attitudes that will result in a change in behavior. Counselors use a variety of techniques to bring this change about, ranging from careful listening (easier said than done) to group sessions; these techniques are described more fully in later chapters.

One seeming fault of the definition is the absence of the word *guidance,* a word long associated with counseling, as seen in the statement by Dr. Herr. The omission is intentional. It was made for two reasons. In the first place, guidance is associated with school counselors, especially high school counselors; this group is becoming a smaller part of the whole. Second, even in schools, counseling is considered the heart of the guidance program.

Counseling as an occupation may not be easily defined, and a fisherman may be unable to show you one. You can, however, look at counselors. Chapters in this book describe four individual counselors in a variety of settings dealing with an assortment of clients in differing ways. Other chapters give information in a more systematic way about the concerns of counselors, their characteristics, and the different approaches they take to their work. Basic facts about these occupations—such as salaries, number employed, and training required—are also included. The next to the last chapter passes on advice from more than a score of working counselors. My hope is that this book will increase your understanding of counselors, their goals, and their options so that you can match their characteristics and aspirations with your own.

Top: A vocational rehabilitation specialist goes over interest inventory and career assessment test results with a client. (Department of Veterans Affairs photo) *Bottom:* This rehabilitation counselor is assessing a client's hand-eye coordination. (photo courtesy of the Rehabilitation Institute of Chicago)

CHAPTER 2

THE VARIETIES OF COUNSELING

In the multitude of counselors there is safety.

—The Bible

Signs of change are everywhere: the guidance office down the school corridor has become a counseling center. Weekly news magazines carry hospital ads for counseling programs that deal with anorexia nervosa and alcoholism. The legislatures in twenty-nine states have passed laws licensing counselors to work outside schools. The National Association of Rehabilitation Professionals in the Private Sector represents several thousand members. And the American Personnel and Guidance Association, the largest professional association in the field, has become the American Association for Counseling and Development (AACD).

Guidance—as will be shown in the chapter on counseling's past—originated in programs that helped people choose careers and soon became tied to schools. It has grown to include counseling on a wide array of concerns and has moved into a variety of settings, including social agencies, major corporations, and private practices.

Becoming a counselor, in other words, will probably offer a person a great many more options in the future than it once did.

Looking back, the transformation of guidance into counseling seems almost inevitable. Just as pioneers clearing new land cut down trees only to discover rocks and boulders, counselors working on the educational and career development of students soon learned that young people had other concerns that a counselor could help with, concerns with family, drug abuse, or normal development. Counselors began to work on these problems in addition to their other duties. Naturally counselors who developed skills in aiding students with such problems could also help others. And so counselors increasingly found positions beyond the schoolhouse door, often specializing in fields such as employment, rehabilitation, or mental health.

TYPES OF COUNSELORS

The total number of counselors exceeded 206,000 in 1988. All the following job titles refer to counselors of one sort or another:

Career counselor
Certified mental health counselor
Child development specialist
College admissions counselor
College counselor
Community agency counselor
Community mental health counselor
Counseling psychologist
Elementary school counselor
Family therapist
Human development counselor
Intervention specialist
Job counselor
Marriage counselor
Marriage, family, and divorce counselor
Mental health counselor
Prison counselor
Professional counselor
Public offender counselor
Rehabilitation counselor
Secondary school counselor
Vocational counselor
Vocational rehabilitation counselor

The number of counselors working outside educational institutions has grown to the point that the nature of their work cannot be described simply in terms of school, even when the change in emphasis in school counseling—from testing and educational programs to the resolution of behavioral concerns—is taken into account. North Carolina's Department of Public Instruction summarizes the universals of counseling when it says a guidance program has three components: learning to live, learning to learn, and learning to make a living.

FUNCTIONS OF COUNSELORS

No matter where they work, counselors use individual and group counseling techniques to help people with a wide range of personal, social, career, and educational needs, according to the American Association of Counseling and Development. As Frank Burtnett said when he was assistant executive director of the Association, "Counselors help people work with a concern before it becomes a problem or crisis." For example, counselors help people deal with stress; examine marital and family conflicts and family communication; adjust and cope with problems created by accident, illness, or other disabling misfortune; and obtain career counseling that takes into account the person's education, training, work history, interest, skills, and aptitudes. Often counselors must administer tests and interpret their results in order to help individuals learn about their strengths, weaknesses, and potential. Generally counselors will concentrate on prevention or development, but some counselors specialize in remedial services. And one of the counselor's most important functions is to refer people to other sources of assistance when their problems are outside the scope of his or her specialized skills.

Another way of describing the functions of a counselor is to say that he or she intervenes to benefit the individual. W.H. Morril, E.R. Oetling, and J.C. Hurst developed a model to show the nature of the interventions counselors make. They note that the target of the intervention can be the individual, the primary group (the people the individual is close to), an associational group (people who share a concern), and the institution or community. The purpose of the intervention may be remediation, prevention, or development. And the method of intervention may be direct service; consultation with and training of people who will work with the individual; or various media, such as announcements, pamphlets, newspaper articles, and computer terminals.

COUNSELING SERVICES AND SETTINGS

The range of services provided by counselors is wide, although individual counselors are specialized. Rehabilitation counselors, for example, help the disabled become self-sufficient. However, to do this, they must first evaluate the client's condition and potential in far more detail than a school counselor usually does. Similarly, employment counselors might suggest specific jobs to a client and contact potential employers rather than provide only the general career information that a student needs. And mental health counselors—the fastest-growing segment of the occupation—must work closely with psychiatrists, psychologists, clinical social workers, and psychiatric nurses on a far more regular basis than does the school-based counselor.

Among the problems that counselors are more likely to deal with outside the schools than in them are physical and vocational rehabilitation, unemployment and underemployment, reentering school or work, parenting, child abuse, marital and family relationships, career changes, retirement, aging, bereavement, institutionalization, and spiritual concerns.

The nature of a counselor's work is conditioned by the work setting; typically, counselors outside the schools do more case work with individuals or small groups than do school counselors. The setting can also present unique problems, of course. For example, everyone in a school will generally have the best interests of the student at heart; a counselor employed by a large corporation, on the other hand, must take both the worker being counseled and the good of the company into account.

Despite the growing numbers of counseling specialties, it should be stressed that the divisions are not watertight. For example, when counselors in community colleges were asked what would benefit them most, the second-most-common response was training in providing career counseling to the mature adult, which is, of course, one of the major concerns of employment counselors. And having the time to perform behavioral counseling would help school counselors prevent problems before they arise.

A counselor's work has many cycles. The day, the week, the year, the individual case history—each has peaks and valleys that shape the occupation. The following chapters each look at a counseling occupation within a different framework: the annual cycle of a high school counselor, a day in the life of an elementary school counselor, a single case history for a rehabilitation counselor in private practice, and an interview with a mental health counselor in private practice. No one of them tells all there is to learn about the nature of counseling. Together, however, they give a fair representation of the major activities of professional counselors.

One of the secondary school counselor's functions is to help students understand the results of aptitude tests. (NCR Corporation photo)

CHAPTER 3

HIGH SCHOOL COUNSELORS: SQUEEZING A YEAR INTO TEN MONTHS

> But where's the man who counsel can bestow, Still pleas'd to teach, and yet not proud to know
> —Alexander Pope

Oakton High School sits surrounded by new developments in one of the fastest-growing areas of the country. It is a major part of the lives of more than twenty-five hundred students—the scene of their triumphs and defeats in athletics and social events as well as academics. For as long as it has existed—about twenty years—Mary Ashton has been a part of it, first as a teacher, then as a counselor, and now as director of guidance services. As director, with eight regular counselors and two secretaries under her supervision, she has more administrative duties than many counselors. Early in the school year, for example, she must review the objectives developed by each regular counselor. Students are assigned to Oakton's counselors alphabetically, so that each counselor works with students from all four grades. Ms. Ashton has found that this arrangement keeps the counselors up to date on the many different kinds of information that the students request. Another advantage of this system is that all the children in a family have the same counselor. Ms. Ashton also assigns special duties to counselors, such as acting as liaison to disabled students or a particular grade level.

In addition to administering the guidance program, Mary Ashton counsels individuals and families, although a review of her annual calendar does not show much of this side of her work. For example, she counsels students who enter the school under special circumstances, such as a return from a mental institution. She also takes over the counseling sessions of staff members who are called into crisis situations. Every referral of a student to therapy or special education classes requires consultation with her. And because she is well known in the neighborhood as a result of her long association with the school, parents sometimes call her directly with concerns that may require counseling.

Although Mary Ashton's duties thus differ somewhat from those of a typical counselor, they still reflect the rhythm of the high school year. Besides, as many would be quick to proclaim, no counselor is typical anyway.

No matter what calendars say, school years begin in the fall, which means August for Mary Ashton. She has the counseling center largely to herself for a couple of weeks before the regular counselors return. During the brief spell between the end of summer school and the beginning of the fall semester, she is concerned with the registration of students who have moved into the district since June, the schedules of students who attended summer school, and the freshman orientation program. She also attends to the needs of rising seniors who plan to apply either to one of the service academies or for ROTC scholarships. These students see her filled with hopeful anxiety. Less hopeful are others who often come into the counseling center at this time of year: former students who dropped out of school before graduating. Most often, returning to high school would be a bad idea for these older students, so Ms. Ashton talks over other possibilities with them, such as taking the GED exam or attending a nearby community college. In many cases she finds that these people have not worked in a field that made full use of their aptitudes, and she is able to direct them toward apprenticeship or other training programs that they would probably find more satisfying than high school academics.

In September, school is in full swing. The counseling staff screens newcomers to identify those who would benefit from special education classes. Counselors also distribute information booklets concerning colleges to the seniors during September and conduct sessions for the juniors on the same subject. Whenever information is given to a group of students, as in these cases, individuals often request conferences to further explore the issue. Parents, too, often confer with Ms. Ashton to discuss their student's placement or future plans.

College plans also bulk large in October, the month when Oakton holds a college fair with exhibits and presentations for three hundred some schools. So many institutions send representatives that students need help deciding which ones to learn about. October is also PSAT month, generating a good deal of what Ms. Ashton calls *administrivia* having to do with room assignments, the recruitment of proctors, and the review of application forms. The PSAT, or Preliminary Scholastic Aptitude Test, is a practice test given to those who plan to take the SAT (Scholastic Aptitude Test) for college admission. While the PSAT is taken mostly by juniors, the freshmen and some seniors also take tests at this time. The freshmen take a differential aptitude test. Some seniors take a minimum competency examination that all Virginia high school students must pass in order to graduate. Students usually pass the exam during their sophomore year, but it must be administered again for those who failed and for students who moved into the state after the exam was last given. Planning for the sophomores' career exploration activities also occurs this month.

All the counseling and administrative tasks related to college admissions continue to require attention during November. While the seniors worry about where they will be next year, many of their youngest classmates—the freshmen—worry about the end of their first high school grading period. The receipt of grades usually triggers a round of conferences with students and parents and some schedule changes.

The counseling center is as busy in December as one of the suburban malls where the students shop. Ms. Ashton reviews the school's curriculum with an assistant principal, passing on ideas from the students and parents. The return of the PSAT scores also causes a flurry of activity. About this time of year, too, the juniors take part in career exploration workshops and other activities.

According to Dick Clark and the crowd in Times Square, one year ends and another begins on January 1, but no change occurs at the counseling center, where the pace won't let up for months. Deadlines for college applications come and go throughout the winter. Periodically the center holds parent coffees in the evening. The semester ends, requiring more conferences and schedule readjustments as well as signaling the beginning of preregistration counseling for the fall semester. Another major event of the month is the after-school meeting on financial aid, which is always of great concern in this school where 80 percent of the students go on for further studies.

By the end of March, minimum competency exams will be given to the sophomores and SRAs to the juniors. The results of these tests, like the results of all the other academic and aptitude assessments made throughout the year, will stimulate visits to the counselors. Events that take place outside the school can also propel people into the center. A television show on incest or teenage suicide, for example, may cause students, their friends, their parents, or their neighbors to contact the counseling center.

April and May largely belong to the juniors, at first glance. A parent night focuses attention on their post-high school plans, and a series of workshops prepares them for applying to colleges. The administration of the college boards and advanced placement exams are particularly time-consuming services. The status of each senior must also be reviewed to ensure that everyone will qualify for graduation. Registration for summer school also takes place throughout this period, a change from the days when students usually took summer school classes to make up for courses that they had failed during the regular school year. Ms. Ashton and members of her staff also visit six different junior highs that feed into Oakton, meeting next year's freshmen and explaining the various educational options open to them.

Paperwork consumes much of Ms. Ashton's time in June. Students take the last of the many examinations they must sit through, and the building quiets down. For two weeks after the end of the semester, the teachers and regular counselors continue to work, winding up one year and planning for the next. Finally, only a few people are left in the building—people like the custodian, the principal, and Mary Ashton. She will have two weeks to tie up loose ends, such as reviewing evaluations from the seniors, and to map out ideas for next year. If she's lucky, she'll have a chance to catch her breath. After all, autumn is just a month away.

CHAPTER 4

ELEMENTARY SCHOOL COUNSELORS: WHAT A DAY!

As the twig . . .

—A Proverb

The afternoon I visited Houston Elementary School, rain fell heavily, greening the grass and quieting this city neighborhood. A bedraggled robin seeking shelter in a rosebush was the liveliest thing around. The school itself was just as quiet, making me conclude wrongly that classes were over for the day; then a bell rang, and the corridor filled with children ready for the school day and the school week to end. As I entered her office, Ellissia Price—the American School Counselor's Association "Counselor of the Year" for 1982–83—was giving some final instructions to four students collating an information package. Here, too, all was quiet and calm, a tribute to how well Ms. Price controls the hectic activities of her day.

Her day began with a stop to drop off applications for some of her students to attend a computer camp—the last step after speaking to students, giving out applications, reminding students to return them, and collecting them. Arriving at school, she called the Bureau of Printing and Engraving to confirm arrangements for a field trip the fifth grade class was to make that day.

Ms. Price's own schedule called for visits to three classes in the morning. Counselors rarely have the luxury of doing only what they plan, however, and today's field trip resulted in a slight adjustment. One of the fifth graders—we'll call him Oliver—would not go with his class.

Nor would he go to the sixth grade for the morning. His teacher asked Ms. Price for assistance. Oliver agreed to spend the morning with the counselor, an offer she had made with some ambivalence because it would reward his poor behavior with her attention.

Ms. Price knows each of the 366 students in her school, of course, but she sees some more frequently than others. Oliver is one of these. The adults in his life have ignored him, and he feels worthless; he lashes out in school, hoping his poor behavior will win the attention that he feels he does not deserve for himself. This morning, Ms. Price would continue her work with Oliver, adding another block and a little more mortar to his slowly growing sense of responsibility and self-respect. He would also perform some little jobs for her, such as distributing to the teachers the cumulative academic, assessment, and health records of all the students.

Before visiting her first class, Ms. Price also had to consult with a teacher concerning a sixth grader we will call Sherry Finn. One of Ms. Price's personal goals this year is to reduce the absentee rate by 5 percent. Reaching the goal has required the cooperation of teachers and parents with whom Ms. Price has spoken on the telephone, in her office, and in their homes. Sherry has been a notable part of the attendance concern. Ms. Price has had numerous conversations with her and visited her home, securing the cooperation of her mother in positive ways. Sherry's attendance has improved a hundred percent this year, but the warmth of spring has led to some relapses.

The sixth grade class is one of several that Ms. Price sees regularly. The others she would visit this morning are a special education class for the trainable retarded in the middle grades (ages eight to thirteen) and one for the educable retarded in the same grades. Today all the classes would deal with occupations and careers.

The sixth graders had asked some questions about the appropriateness of different jobs for boys and girls—perhaps it would be more true to say that they had expressed some convictions about the proper place for men and women in the world of work, convictions that have little to do with the reality of our society. Ms. Price used a selection from *Free to Be You and Me* as a springboard for discussion. Although the class seemed to deal only with careers, Ms. Price's ultimate aim was to show that the individual must exercise free and responsible choice in every facet of life.

Group guidance activities such as this cover many subjects, including substance abuse, stranger danger, and child abuse. Sometimes teachers ask Ms. Price to conduct such sessions on a continuing basis. Other times she will suggest holding one, such as when a teacher's evaluations of individual students indicate that a whole class has become unruly. In such a situation, no border can be placed between group guidance and group counseling.

In today's other classes, Ms. Price showed a film about the occupations of workers in a school. She then took the educable class to visit the office and the janitor to reinforce what they had seen so that they could relate the film to the people in their own lives. The trainable students, after seeing the film, drew pictures of people in the various occupations. These different strategies for the three classes are a reminder of the flexibility that Ms. Price must bring to her tasks. She must regularly devise appropriate techniques for dealing with the great variety of concerns of students who fall on every point of the developmental curve, from the slow-learning preschooler to the intellectually superior sixth grader.

At 12:30 on this rainy Friday, Ms. Price went to the kindergarten class and played shape bingo. Once again, an apparently simple activity will do double or even triple duty. The sessions with the kindergarten children and others provide Ms. Price with the opportunity of observing the students without being noticed. During them, she can watch how they interact, identifying those who would benefit from individual counseling. She can also evaluate the students' behavior and skills, using her personal observations to confirm or challenge the results of the formal assessments that she administers. The sessions also serve to increase her visibility so that the students will know her and feel more comfortable about coming to see her. For the children, however, the game is merely fun; they realize neither how important recognizing basic shapes will be to their reading ability nor how much Ms. Price is learning about them.

The afternoon—is it really only afternoon?—began with teacher conferences concerning referrals for special education programs. But once again a student's behavior interrupted Ms. Price's plans. Andrew Kensley, a fourth grader, had threatened another student in such a way as to trigger reaction from the teacher. Andy, too, was a continuing counselee for Ms. Price. His behavior had worsened recently. It appeared that his stepfather had lost his job and that the family was under great stress. Hoping to have a private conference with Andy's mother, Ms. Price had recently accompanied him home at the end of the school day. Unfortunately, his stepfather was also home that afternoon.

When the last bell rang for the students, Ms. Price still had much to do. For one thing, she was going to talk to me. More typical was her schedule for the previous Friday when she led a session of the Junior Beta Club, a service organization for the sixth graders. Unbeknownst to the students, Ms. Price was developing their decision-making skills by way of a discussion of what to do for the school volunteers at the end of the year. She set the parameters for the gifts—time and money—and led a brainstorming session on gift ideas. Eventually the club members decided to make lollipop corsages similar to a candy corsage one of the students had seen in a florist's window.

Another after-school session that day promised to be more challenging. The parents of three students—two of them under the age of six—were breaking up. Ms. Price was going to meet with the children, just as she would meet with the parents when asked. She would help the youngsters talk about their reaction to the separation by using a feeling board—a large picture that shows children experiencing certain key emotions such as anger, loneliness, fear, and joy. All Ms. Price's training as a counselor would be called upon in learning the meaning behind some of the children's comments.

By the time I left Houston School, the rain had let up, and the water-slick grass looked shellacked in the gray light of the afternoon. A fat worm that had fled its water-soaked hole rewarded the robin for her discomfort during the downpour. The students from Houston were nowhere to be seen. Few of them, probably, remembered their encounters with Ellissia Price that day. Within them, however, the subconscious memory of her lessons would continue to work, helping each of them to consider all the options life offers and to value properly their own worth.

CHAPTER 5

REHABILITATION: FROM ASSESSMENT TO EMPLOYMENT

> Blessed is he who has found his work; let him ask no other blessedness.
>
> —Thomas Carlyle

Francis Thomas has been counseling the disabled for fifteen years. Although, like many rehabilitation counselors, he began his career working for a state agency, he is now president of Comprehensive Career Evaluative Services, Inc., a private rehabilitation firm that provides vocational counseling, alcohol counseling, job placement, and staff development training. He is a member of the National Rehabilitation Association and president of the Chesapeake Association of Rehabilitation Professionals in the Private Sector. He also finds time in his busy professional schedule to continue his doctoral studies at the University of Maryland.

The motto, "Above all, do no harm," governs Mr. Thomas's practice; to him, it means that clients should be no worse off at the end of the rehabilitation period than they were before becoming disabled. Among other things, that means they should not suffer a great loss in earning power because of their change of occupation. The case history of one of his recent clients—whose name is not the one used here—shows how Mr. Thomas puts his counseling philosophy into practice. The initial interview might have gone like this.

> Charlie Hartsman eyed the counselor suspiciously. Charlie had collected worker's compensation for a year and a half. Finally, the worker's

compensation board had referred him to Francis Thomas for rehabilitation counseling. Mr. Thomas, large of frame and agile of motion, was all that Charlie would never be again. "Now what?" he thought. Would he soon be able to take charge of his own life again? Was this just a delaying tactic by the board? Was he going to be pushed into a dead-end, minimum-wage job? At least he'd find out soon.

"Good morning, Mr. Hartsman."

"Hi."

"I've looked over your records. I see you injured your back unloading bags of coins for the transit company. Would you like to return to work for them?"

"Yeah. I guess so. You know, I've got some years with them and the retirement and what not. But, you know, they've acted like *I owe them* for messin' up my back, you know what I mean?"

"You feel they haven't been fair to you?"

"Right. Like, I didn't *try* to get hurt, you know what I mean?"

"The way they've handled this, they've put the blame on you."

"Yeah. They're not the only place to work. Still, I do have some years in, like I said."

"Even though you don't like the way the company treated you, you would not mind going back to work for it because of things like your seniority, health insurance, and pension."

"That's right."

"Well, when you were working, did you notice any jobs you'd like?"

"I dunno. Maybe bus checker, the guy who stands at a bus stop and checks what time each bus gets there and how many people are on it and stuff."

The initial interview continues with the counselor moving toward several goals. He must show that he has the client's best interest at heart and establish a counseling relationship. Clients may direct considerable anger and frustration at the counselor during the initial interview or later in their rehabilitation program. By the time clients see a counselor, the reality of their disability has begun to sink in. Because of the length of time that often elapses between the date of the injury and the first session with the counselor, clients may also feel that they have not been treated fairly. On the other hand, some clients may have become adjusted to receiving worker's compensation, which can amount to three-fourths of their previous salary, and see the counselor as a threat to their new way of life.

An additional challenge for the counselor is to get the clients to make their own decisions. The counselor represents authority to many clients, and they are ready to do whatever they are told so they don't lose their benefits. In many cases, the same client will exhibit each of these tendencies—anger, rebellion, and docility—at different times.

After the interview, Mr. Thomas contacted the transit company concerning the bus checker position. He forwarded Charlie's records to them for review. While the company reviewed the case, Mr. Thomas saw his client regularly, providing supportive counseling.

As it turned out, the company would not reemploy Charlie as a checker because the job required being out of doors in all types of weather. It suggested that an indoor job, such as bookkeeping, was a better possibility. Upon receiving this information, Mr. Thomas conducted a counseling session to learn Charlie's reaction to the turn of events. Charlie thought the job might work out, although he would need at least a year of training to qualify for it. In fact, he had wanted to continue his schooling before he went to work, but family circumstances prevented it.

The worker's compensation board would have to approve a training allotment in order for Charlie to attend school, so securing one would be the next order of business. While the board was considering the request, Mr. Thomas explored various school programs with Charlie. Eventually, arrangements were made for him to attend a local business college.

The Hartsman case was more or less on hold during the training period. Francis Thomas continued to provide supportive counseling, seeing his client at least once a month and speaking to him weekly; Mr. Thomas also filed monthly reports to the board. All in all, the case appeared to be heading toward a favorable outcome.

But then some flies showed up in the ointment. Toward the end of the year, the company reported to Mr. Thomas that no position would be available. After another round of discussions, Charlie decided to continue in the training program and earn his associate's degree.

Yet another year passed. At the end of it, Charlie finally went back to work. He still is not working in the accounting department, however, although he has been promised the first job that becomes available.

In some ways, Charlie Hartsman was an easy client to work with. He was not subject to severe depression nor did he become dependent on drugs or alcohol after his injury. Furthermore, he was willing to work indoors at a desk job, working conditions that appear intolerable to many of the formerly active disabled. He also had an aptitude for accounting and wanted to go back to school. Still, the case took more than three years to resolve, hardly a short time in a person's life.

At the end of those three years, however, Francis Thomas had more than the satisfaction of knowing that he had done no harm. He had taken an unskilled client with a back injury and returned him to the labor force with the promise of a good career in a field full of opportunities for professional advancement.

CHAPTER 6

MENTAL HEALTH COUNSELORS IN PRIVATE PRACTICE: AN INTERVIEW

> We are not ourselves when nature, being oppressed, commands the mind to suffer with the body.
>
> —Shakespeare

How do you catch a wave upon the shore? How do you pin down a person who wears so many hats? Dr. Linda Seligman is a counselor educator at George Mason University in Virginia, a consultant to the Department of Corrections in Maryland's Montgomery County, and a counselor in private practice, working out of an office in her home. She also conducts workshops and has numerous publications, including *Assessment in Developmental Career Counseling* and *Diagnosis and Treatment Planning in Counseling*.

I caught up with Dr. Seligman at her office on the George Mason campus one Monday between semesters. With so much to discuss and so little time, the conversation jumped quickly from topic to topic. We began with questions appropriate to the university setting.

Q: What do you teach?

A: I teach a variety of courses, including the techniques of diagnosis and treatment planning, couples and family counseling, an introductory course on the theories and techniques of counseling, group counseling, career counseling, and counseling in agency, business, and government settings. I also supervise students during their practicums and internships.

Q: Your work with the Department of Corrections must be very different from teaching.
A: Yes, it is, although I'm relying on the same expertise both as a teacher and as a consultant.
Q: What do you do for the department?
A: I work with the staff at a halfway house. When new residents arrive, for example, I assist with the initial interview. I also consult with the staff as needed when special difficulties occur with an individual's adjustment.
Q: Combining the roles of educator and consultant would seem to give you a very diverse range of duties. Why did you also enter into private practice?
A: Well, private practice gives me the opportunity to assist a different population. It is also a response to the needs of individuals in the community.
Q: How do your clients find you? Are they referred to you by other practitioners?
A: Actually they are more often referred by other clients. One of my clients, for example, was a high school senior who was suffering from depression and having problems adjusting to certain conditions in her life. She began seeing me at the suggestion of a friend whose family I was counseling. Another former client suggested that a woman she knew who had very low self-esteem come to talk with me. As it turned out, the woman had concerns about her life goals, complicated by marital difficulties. During that same period, I was counseling a woman who had never married and was experiencing a mid-life crisis. You might say she referred herself to me after attending an assertiveness workshop that I lead. As you can see, the practice pretty much builds on itself.
Q: Was it always like that?
A: I'd say so. At the very beginning—but after I had gained many years of experience—I simply placed ads in the telephone directory and some other places. Since then—that was 1975—I've not had any shortage of people to fill the six to ten hours a week that I'm able to devote to private practice.

Q: Many of us know about counselors only because of career exploration activities they conducted when we were in high school. Career concerns don't seem to enter into your private practice, though. Is that true?

A: Perhaps I should say yes and no. Career concerns have been relevant to many of my clients, including those who are developing a clearer awareness of their goals in life and those going through a mid-life crisis. Clients may also come to me with questions about appropriate careers. I'll review their academic experience with them, use instruments such as the Strong-Campbell Interest Inventory, and practice other techniques to help them clarify their options. Sometimes, of course, clients ask career questions as a point of entry; their real problems may turn out to be social adjustment, family conflict, or any number of other problems.

Q: How about payment? Is that difficult to arrange?

A: No. Basically, my clients pay me and are then, often, reimbursed by their insurance company, depending on the policy they have. Of course the company may be more willing to pay for my services because I am a licensed psychologist than they would be for an unlicensed counselor.

Before Dr. Seligman had finished her last comment, my time was up. Her conversation had started many a rabbit I wished I could pursue—the outcomes of the counseling she had performed, the most challenging cases, the drawbacks of the field. Now, however, she had to turn her attention to her other duties. The wave cannot linger on the shore.

Top: Some of the techniques elementary school counselors may use include play, drawing, and storytelling. (Cedarville College photo) *Bottom:* This counselor, who is a sign language expert, leads a group session for deaf high school students. (Chicago Department of Health photo)

CHAPTER 7

SCHOOL COUNSELORS: FACTS AND FIGURES

OTHER JOB TITLES

Guidance counselor, adjustment counselor, crisis resource teacher, career guidance counselor, guidance director, learning specialist, middle school/junior high school counselor, elementary school counselor, intervention specialist, child development specialist.

GOALS AND DUTIES

Help students understand themselves, clarify the opportunities available to them, and reach their goals.

School counselors have at least seven general duties: counseling students or others; consulting with parents, teachers, administrators, and other student personnel workers such as school psychologists and social workers; appraising the abilities and aptitudes of students through tests and other procedures; informing students and others concerning the school's programs, other educational programs, employment opportunities, and the availability of social services; referring students or other counselees to more specialized avenues of counseling or treatment; administering the guidance program; and conducting research or continuing their own education.

The following services are offered by a typical guidance department: orientation of new students; assignment of students to classes; provision of information and counseling for students individually and in groups concerning study skills, educational plans, career plans, employment opportunities, financial aid, behavioral difficulties, social development, and personal problems; consultation with administrators, teachers, and parents concerning the educational, vocational, social, and personal development of individual students and the student body as a whole; training of administrators, teachers, and parents to work with students more effectively; scheduling, administering, and explaining the results of aptitude, ability, and interest tests for individuals and groups; keeping records of students' academic work, extracurricular activities, goals, accomplishments, attendance, and reasons for leaving school; and placement of students in employment in or outside the school.

The amount of time an individual counselor spends on any single activity is subject to enormous variation, largely because of administrative decisions made by the school principal or school board. In the words of Dr. Edwin L. Herr, testifying before the U.S. Senate, "What school counselors do is ultimately shaped by the characteristics of the local school districts in which they are employed." Counselors would prefer to spend most of their time in consultant and counselor roles, with the balance spent on research and the administration of the guidance program.

Counselors in the schools are not the only ones who provide pupil services. Other members of the pupil services team may include a psychologist, social worker, nurse, and attendance officer. Several of these occupations are discussed in the chapter on other counseling-related occupations. Admissions, housing, student activities, financial aid, and religious activities also fall under pupil services. The duties of a counselor depend in part on how a school district uses these other personnel.

The kind of work counselors do in the schools also depends in part on the grade of the students served: secondary, elementary, or middle and junior high school students.

SECONDARY SCHOOL COUNSELORS

According to the College Entrance Examination Board's Commission on Precollege Guidance and Counseling, "The school counselor should be first and foremost an educator, supporting students in their progress through the school and serving as a crucial resource for the academic program." Secondary school counselors generally deal with four types of subjects or concerns: educational, vocational, social, and personal.

Educational concerns range from freshman orientation (an information function), to administering entrance examinations (an appraisal function), to helping a student sort out the advantages and disadvantages of various postsecondary programs (a counseling function). Personal concerns might be dealt with through a group guidance arrangement (such as a workshop on time management and study skills) or either individual or group counseling (such as a group of the friends of a student who committed suicide).

The following role statement for secondary school counselors from the American School Counselor Association will be revised during 1989, but it still captures the counselor's duties:

- Organize and implement through interested teachers guidance curricula interventions that focus upon important developmental concerns of adolescents (identity, career choice and planning, social relationships, and so forth).
- Organize and make available comprehensive information systems (print, computer based, audiovisual) necessary for educational-vocational planning and decision making.
- Assist students with assessment of personal characteristics (e.g., competencies, interests, aptitudes, needs, career maturity) for personal use in such areas as course selection, post-high school planning, and career choices.
- Provide remedial interventions or alternative programs for those students showing in-school adjustment problems, vocational immaturity, or general negative attitudes toward personal growth.

In a single week's work, a secondary school counselor might have a conference with several teachers concerning a student's behavior, process an application for a student's part-time job, meet with the principals of the high school and middle school to make plans for the orientation of next year's freshmen, consult with a parent about a student's adjustment to a new family situation, help a student understand the results of an aptitude test, lead a group session for the friends of a student who committed suicide, administer an academic achievement test to the sophomore class, help a group of seniors decide which colleges to apply for, and show some juniors how to use a computer terminal to find out about different careers.

Typically, of course, the work would be far less varied. In many schools, for example, a counselor would work with only one class rather than all four. In others, a counselor will work with the ninth and eleventh grades one year and the tenth and twelfth grades the next, an arrangement that gives students the advantage of continuity and counselors the advantage of variety.

Not all counselors find their jobs so multifaceted. Some complain that they are little more than office clerks handling academic transcripts, schedule changes, school applications, attendance registers, and administrative duties. Surveys have found that many secondary school counselors spend one-third to two-thirds of their time on relatively routine paperwork or registration activities.

ELEMENTARY SCHOOL COUNSELORS

Elementary school counselors report doing more counseling and more consulting with teachers, administrators, and parents than secondary school counselors do. As much as 80 percent of the elementary school counselor's time may be spent in these activities, with about half that time spent with students and much of the rest with teachers. Educational and vocational concerns take up relatively little of the elementary school counselor's time, while social and personal concerns take relatively more than is the case in secondary schools. In addition, the techniques of counseling an elementary school pupil differ markedly from those used with adolescents. For example, play, drawing, and storytelling may be utilized simply to learn the nature of the pupil's concern.

The following role statement from the American School Counselor Association sums up the duties of elementary school counselors:
- Provide in-service training to teachers to assist them with planning and implementing guidance interventions for young children (preschool to third grade) in order to maximize developmental benefits (self-esteem, personal relationship, positive school attitudes, and so forth) in the hope of preventing serious problems or minimizing the size of such problems if and when they do occur.
- Provide consultations for teachers who need help understanding and incorporating developmental concepts in teacher content as well as support for building a healthy classroom environment.
- Accommodate parents who need assistance with understanding normal child growth and development and their role in encouraging their child to learn as well as improving family communication skills.
- Cooperate with other school staff in the early identification, remediation, or referral of children with developmental deficiencies or handicaps.
- As children reach the upper elementary grades, effort is directed through the curriculum toward increasing student awareness of the relationship between school and work, especially the impact of educational choices on one's life-style and career development.

MIDDLE AND JUNIOR HIGH SCHOOL COUNSELORS

Students in middle and junior high schools are often spoken of as *transescent,* or in transition from childhood to adolescence. The duties of counselors who work in these schools, therefore, might be expected to resemble a cross between the duties of elementary school and secondary school counselors. They do.

Junior high school counselors in one study reported spending 85 percent of their time counseling. Counselors in another study reported spending 50 to 60 percent of their time counseling students in regard to improving interpersonal relationships, values clarification, crises such as death and divorce, and the physical, emotional, and other changes of puberty. Counselors in this study also reported spending 10 to 25 percent of their time coordinating services to the student, 10 to 20 percent as consultants working with teachers or other adults who deal with the students, and 2 to 33 percent as curriculum specialists conducting in-service training, group guidance for students on subjects such as human sexuality or career education, and parent education programs.

The American School Counselor Association has developed the following role statement for middle and junior high school counselors:

- Concentrate efforts...to smooth the transition of the student from the [lower school to the middle or junior high school].
- Identify, encourage, and support teachers (through in-service training, consultation, and coteaching) who are interested in incorporating developmental units in [their curriculums].
- Organize and implement a career guidance program that includes an assessment of [each student's] career maturity and career-planning status; easy access to relevant career information; and assistance with processing data for personal use in schoolwork-related decision making.

EMPLOYMENT AND OUTLOOK

According to the U.S. Department of Education, there were 68,500 counselors in the public schools in the fall of 1986. The Department does not distinguish employment by level, but a survey conducted by the American Association of Counseling and Development's library found that there were almost sixteen thousand elementary school counselors in 1987–88. According to many experts, the job market is currently good for prospective counselors. The outlook for the future is also promising.

Although the job outlook for school counselors differs greatly by the educational level of the students served, the data available do not permit such an analysis. It is possible, however, to project the demand for school counselors in general and then comment on probable trends at the different levels. The demand for counselors is determined by three factors: the number of students, the ratio of counselors to students, and the number of working counselors who leave the occupation.

In the fall of 1986, there were almost forty million students in public elementary and secondary schools, according to the U.S. Department of Education. These schools employed 68,500 counselors, or about 1 counselor for every 580 students; most private high schools also employ counselors. The Department projects a public school enrollment of almost forty-four million in 1997. To maintain the same ratio of counselors to students, therefore, would require an additional 7,800 counselors, an increase of 12 percent. Population projections from the Bureau of the Census indicate little change between 1997 and 2000. Those projections do make clear, however, that increased immigration could push the demand for counselors higher. Demand would also be higher if schools try to reduce the ratio of counselors to students, as was the trend in the first half of the 1980s. Between 1979 and 1986, the number of counselors rose 10 percent even though enrollments declined by 1.8 million; during that same period, the number of teachers rose only 3 percent.

Important as growth can be to an occupation, it usually accounts for only a small fraction of total openings. This is certainly the case in counseling. Most jobs become available because of turnover, which occurs when people in an occupation leave it. The separation rate for all counselors was 11 percent in 1986. Even if the rate for school counselors was lower than other counseling occupations, it would probably be somewhere between 7 percent (the rate for educational administrators) and 9 percent (the rate for secondary school teachers); the rate for elementary school teachers was 12 percent. Depending on the actual separation rate, turnover makes five to eight thousand openings available a year; in other words, more openings occur in one year because of turnover than in ten because of growth. And indications are that the separation rate of counselors may rise. A large percentage of counselors may soon retire; 30 to 50 percent of the counselors in some school districts will become eligible for retirement in the next five years. In Ohio, one-fourth of the counselors had twenty-four years or more of experience in education in 1987.

The supply of people to fill these openings comes from two sources: experienced counselors not currently in the occupation and new recipients of master's degrees. People in the field say that shortages are likely and that they might even be severe in states or school districts that are growing rapidly or that are reducing their student-counselor ratios. The available data generally support this view, although difficulties with classification make only rough comparisons possible. For example, about one-fourth of the twenty-one thousand people who became counselors during 1987 were reentering the occupation, according to the U.S. Department of Labor; but it is not clear how many of these counselors worked in schools. By comparison, only 9 percent of the entering psychologists were experienced, whereas 35 percent of the high school teachers were. Data on the number of degrees awarded are also difficult to analyze. About nine thousand master's degrees are awarded each year for school counselors. This number would seem to be large enough to generate a surplus, but another survey indicates that approximately the same number of new master's degree recipients were placed in school counselor positions in 1985.

While firm projections of the demand for counselors by grade level are not possible, certain trends can be identified. High school enrollments are projected to rise 15 percent from 1989 to 1997 by the U.S. Department of Education. Such a rise would increase employment of counselors by a similar percentage. Employment would rise more quickly if counselor-student ratios are reduced. This is not likely in the near future, however. In fact, although some school districts have far too many students per counselor and some rural students have no access to a counselor at all, the ratio of high school counselors to high school students is fairly close to the 1 to 250 sought. The situation would change, of course, if money were actually provided to conduct the kinds of programs that are sometimes recommended to combat alcohol and drug abuse, teenage pregnancies, and other problems faced by young people. Turnover among high school counselors will, however, provide thousands of openings.

Elementary enrollments are projected to rise only 6 percent. The employment of elementary school counselors is likely to rise faster than this, however. A book on guidance services published in 1967 stated that the greatest potential for the development of guidance was at the elementary level. The statement is still true. The number of elementary school counselors is far below the recommended level. According to the American Association for Counseling and Development, there were 15,800 elementary school counselors employed in 1987–88. Enrollment was approximately twenty-five million students, giving a ratio of 1 counselor to 1,733 students. The recommended ratio is one to five hundred. There is, therefore, considerable room for growth in the occupation simply to achieve the recommended ratio. Many school districts and several states have recently begun to employ counselors in the elementary schools. But actual growth is still likely to be far slower than potential growth since it is closely tied to tax revenues and expenditures for public schools. In all probability, therefore, growth will be substantial in school districts committed to elementary school guidance programs and minimal in school districts that do not stress such activities.

SALARY, OTHER BENEFITS, AND WORKING CONDITIONS

According to Educational Research Service, the average salary for school counselors was $32,896 a year in 1987–88. Salaries ranged from a low of $26,564 to a high of $37,097. Counselors, therefore, earn somewhat more than classroom teachers, in part because they must have more education and experience to qualify for entry-level positions. They enjoy the usual fringe benefits of teachers, such as health insurance and pension plans.

Generally, the work year for school counselors either matches the school year or runs a month longer, starting two weeks before the beginning of the first term and finishing two weeks after the end of the last term. Although work hours conform to the school day, more or less, counselors often conduct special programs or hold office hours in the evening for students or parents who want to drop by.

Secondary school counselors usually have offices that ensure privacy. Counselors in elementary schools built before guidance programs for the lower grades originated may have makeshift office space. Clerical assistance is inadequate for some counselors.

ENTRY REQUIREMENTS AND CAREER LADDER

The requirements for certification as a school counselor are established by each state independently; in other words, this meat loaf has fifty recipes. A master's degree in counseling or guidance is almost universally a condition of employment. More than three hundred graduate schools have programs that prepare counselors with titles such as guidance, counseling, elementary school guidance, and pupil personnel services. They are usually in the counselor education department of a school of education. The degree entails from thirty to sixty semester hours of course work; fifteen hours in a semester is considered a full schedule. A practicum lasting one hundred to six hundred hours of contact with clients may also be compulsory. Most states also require one to three years of teaching experience, although several now allow the substitution of counseling experience for teaching experience. If a state calls for teaching experience, a prospective counselor must first qualify for teacher certification, which usually requires a set number of education courses taken as an undergraduate or in graduate school and a supervised teaching practicum. Provisional certification may be available for counselors who have not completed their graduate programs. Certification granted by one state will probably not be automatically recognized by another state. A list of state accrediting agencies that can provide detailed information appears in appendix C.

Counselors are at the top of their profession. They may change occupations, however, to increase their earnings, gain more administrative responsibility, or be free to do more specialized work. Counselors can become directors of guidance, counseling, or student personnel services or school administrators; additional graduate-school work in school administration is usually required. Counselors can become professors in counselor education programs; a doctorate is usually required. They may enter private practice, which might require additional certification. And they may become school psychologists or enter related occupations; again, additional education, possibly including a doctorate, is usually mandatory. A survey of graduates of a National Defense Education Act institute for elementary school counselors showed that a few were still counselors thirteen years later, but others had become administrators, social workers, counselors in non-elementary school settings, professors in counselor education programs, or psychological examiners. Some had returned to teaching. Other surveys confirm these findings.

More information about this occupation is available from the associations and in the books and journals listed in appendixes A and B. You should also contact the department of education or public instruction in your state government to learn the certification requirements. State affiliates of national associations such as the American Association for Counseling and Development and the National Education Association may also have useful information.

A NOTE ON INDEPENDENT EDUCATIONAL CONSULTANTS

Some counselors have established private practices that focus on educational placements for high school or college students or students in need of special education. Private practice for this type of counseling is still quite rare; it employs only about five hundred people full time, according to the Independent Educational Consultants Association. People in private practice usually work alone but may have two or three associates, each of whom has a specialty. For example, one associate might have experience teaching in Europe and be familiar with educational placement overseas; another might concentrate on students who need special education.

Often a private educational counselor will act as a consultant to a mental health counselor or psychiatrist who is seeking an educational program for a client. Other clients seek more individual attention than can be provided by a high school counselor. The educational counselor meets with the client and parents, collects information on the client's educational history, aptitudes, financial resources, and educational goals, and tries to make an optimum placement.

Independent educational counselors are not burdened by the administrative duties of school counselors, but school counselors are not burdened with hiring office personnel and collecting fees. Typically, independent counselors have ten to fifteen years experience before entering private practice. Their earnings are comparable to those of school counselors.

More information, specifically a directory of members, is available from the Independent Educational Consultants Association, Cove Road, P.O. Box 125, Forestdale, Massachusetts 02644, (508) 477-2127.

CHAPTER 8

MENTAL HEALTH COUNSELORS: FACTS AND FIGURES

OTHER JOB TITLES

Marriage counselor; family therapist; marriage, family, and divorce counselor; community agency counselor.

GOALS AND DUTIES

Assisting people in coping with problems.

The range of goals and duties for these counselors matches the complete range for all counselors. The client's concerns can range from a child's difficulties in adjusting to a divorce to an older person's anxiety about entering a nursing home. Alcohol and drug abuse, family conflicts, child and spouse abuse, difficulty at work, criminal behavior, and changes in family status are among the problems confronted. Besides providing individual and group counseling, these counselors coordinate treatment plans, administer programs to improve mental health conditions in the community, and intervene in crisis situations.

EMPLOYMENT AND OUTLOOK

Employment probably exceeds fifty thousand, indicating that no counseling specialty has more practitioners. That figure is only an educated guess, however, derived from taking the number of people identified as counselors in one federal survey (206,000) and subtracting from it the probable numbers of school, rehabilitation, employment, and college counselors. It is comparable to rough estimates made by the American Association for Counseling and Development, using the thirteen-thousand-strong membership of its mental health division as a foundation.

The ways used to count the number of people who work in an occupation break down fairly completely for this one. The difficulty, as usual, is lack of agreement as to who works in the occupation. Among those who could be counted as mental health counselors are ministers, priests, and rabbis, who spend much of their time counseling members of their congregation, and people with doctorates in psychology who would usually be considered psychologists. Marriage and family therapists, another closely related occupation, may also be counted among mental health counselors by some; they number twelve thousand or more.

Employers of mental health counselors include mental health clinics, educational institutions, community agencies, social service agencies, prisons, group homes, drug rehabilitation programs, and health maintenance organizations. The National Institutes of Health surveys employment in psychiatric hospitals, clinics, and other facilities. Because employers rarely distinguish between psychologists and counselors, the survey does not provide data for counselors as such. However, the category "other mental health workers" rose dramatically from seventeen thousand in 1976 to fifty-eight thousand in 1986; this category includes various therapists and may include counselors. Another ten thousand or so mental health counselors work in private practice. In addition, many counselor educators and counselors employed by community agencies have part-time private practices.

More than half the graduates of counselor education programs now go into community and agency work. Most say, however, that the total number of graduates with this specialty is about the same as the number of positions available, in part because of a drop in the number of graduates. Others say that the field is still competitive. In all probability, the success of graduates in finding positions depends in part on the reputation of the school they attend and their willingness to relocate.

This occupation is expected to grow faster than average over the next ten years. The major uncertainty in determining the rate of growth is related to the issue of third-party payment. Over the past few years, many insurance plans have reduced the amount of money they will pay for mental health services, and this has acted as a brake on the growth of mental health occupations. At the same time, however, insurers have begun to authorize the payment of counselors for services once performed by psychologists. Should this trend continue, the employment of counselors will continue to grow. The need for these services is clearly expanding, although the willingness of insurance companies to pay for them might not.

SALARY, OTHER BENEFITS, AND WORKING CONDITIONS

The range of salaries naturally matches the range of employers. The earnings of almost all mental health counselors would fall within the $11,000 to $50,000 range. Earnings of counselors in private practice depend largely on the number of hours worked. Typically, the hourly fee charged by counselors in private practice in 1988 was between $40 and $75 for individual counseling and $25 to $40 for group sessions, according to a survey of members of the American Mental Health Counselors Association; the number of sessions held per week varied so widely that the average would not be representative.

Mental health counselors employed by public agencies receive the same fringe benefits as other government workers, including group health insurance, retirement plans, and sick leave. Benefits at community agencies are usually comparable. Counselors in private practice are responsible for their own medical insurance, liability insurance, and pensions.

ENTRY REQUIREMENTS AND CAREER LADDER

The usual educational requirement is a master's degree in counseling for a community or agency setting. Graduates of longer programs that require three hundred or more hours of supervised counseling experience are preferred. These positions are also held by graduates of master's, doctorate, and certificate programs in marriage and family therapy, psychology, or social work.

Advancement can take the form of increased specialization in a particular type of counseling—such as spouse abuse—or increased administrative duties in an agency.

Certification and licensure for counselors is discussed in the chapter on current issues; the situation is changing rapidly. At the moment, certification for counselors in these positions is granted by several bodies.

The National Academy of Certified Clinical Mental Health Counselors administers a specialized certification procedure, while the National Board for Certified Counselors grants a generic certification. Both are affiliated with the American Association for Counseling and Development, 5999 Stevenson Avenue, Alexandria, Virginia 22304, (703) 823-9800.

The American Association of Sex Educators, Counselors, and Therapists (11 Dupont Circle, NW, Suite 220, Washington, D.C. 20036) has separate certification requirements for sex counselors and sex therapists as well as educators and supervisors.

A state license to practice is required in twenty-nine states, with the number increasing. Marriage and family therapists must be licensed in eighteen states. Addresses for both kinds of licensing boards are in appendix C. All the states license psychologists; the American Psychological Association (1200 Seventeenth Street, NW, Washington, D.C. 20036) can provide a list of addresses.

More information about mental health counselors is available from many of the agencies and associations listed in appendix A as well as in most general books on counseling. Registers of certified or licensed counselors and listings in the classified telephone directory can lead you to practicing counselors with whom you can discuss the occupation.

CHAPTER 9

REHABILITATION COUNSELORS: FACTS AND FIGURES

OTHER JOB TITLES

Vocational rehabilitation counselor.

GOALS AND DUTIES

Assisting the disabled to become employed or to lead fuller lives.

Rehabilitation counselors interview a client and administer tests to determine a plan of services to provide. They identify suitable occupations for the client. They provide vocational counseling, including identifying suitable occupations, and assist clients in adjusting to their disabilities, a task that can require the total range of a counselor's skills. Job placement—which may depend on modifications suggested by the counselor—is the ultimate goal for more than 70 percent of all clients. Related duties include case management, the coordination of vocational, medical, and psychological services, provision of financial maintenance, and professional development.

Individual counselors may specialize on a single facet of the occupation, such as cultivating good relations with potential employers, or on a single disability.

Rehabilitation services are provided by state agencies to the deaf, blind, mobility impaired, emotionally disabled, and mentally retarded. Government programs also provide rehabilitation counseling for recovering alcoholics, drug addicts, and prisoners. Recipients of worker's compensation also qualify for rehabilitation services in many states. Typically, these services are provided by private companies or private practitioners who are paid by insurance companies.

A counselor's case load can range from 20 to 150 clients; about 17 percent of the cases can be closed in three months or less, while more than 40 percent take more than a year to resolve. Clients may be referred to the counselor by hospitals, doctors, educational institutions, insurance companies, and worker's compensation boards.

Duties of counselors differ somewhat depending on whether they work for a government agency or a private firm. For example, more than 40 percent of the clients of rehabilitation counselors are mentally ill or retarded; generally, however, only counselors with state agencies are likely to have clients with these conditions. The 20 percent or so of clients suffering from impaired use of a limb or amputation, however, are more likely to receive counseling through an insurance or worker's compensation program. Counselors in public agencies often deal with more severe handicaps and disabilities and have larger case loads. They must also seek remedies for barriers to employment of the handicapped and disabled such as inaccessibility to wheelchairs.

EMPLOYMENT AND OUTLOOK

The employment of rehabilitation counselors exceeds twenty thousand. Counselors employed by the state work in agencies for the handicapped or disabled, mental health institutions, hospitals, schools, and penal institutions. Between seven thousand to nine thousand counselors work in the private sector. Private firms vary widely in size, ranging from one-person operations to companies that employ sixty or more full-time counselors. The Department of Veterans Affairs employs 170 counselors, classified as counseling psychologists.

Overall, this occupation has recently been growing at the rapid rate of about 10 percent a year, almost all of it in the private sector. This private-sector growth is expected to continue, along with slight growth in state agencies.

Employment growth in private companies depends on state laws. Typically, when a state first makes rehabilitation a mandatory part of its worker's compensation laws, employment of rehabilitation counselors in private companies grows very rapidly. Some contraction may then take place as the laws are modified. Eventually, a slow but steady rate of growth is attained.

Currently, rehabilitation counselors enjoy a very favorable job market. One counselor educator estimates that positions could be found for three to five times as many people as are currently completing graduate programs. A large number of vacancies exist in state agencies, although some of these may be due to restrictions on hiring rather than the absence of qualified candidates.

The future is also bright, according to numerous experts. Besides openings due to continued growth, the need to replace counselors who leave the occupation will account for many jobs. This occupation has a surprisingly high turnover rate, especially considering the extensive education required. Much of the turnover, according to several people in the field, results from the ability of counselors to move to more attractive positions with other agencies or to become administrators. The shortage of fully qualified counselors and necessity of hiring people with only a bachelor's degree also explains some of the turnover, however. It is thought that some of these people are dissatisfied with their jobs because they failed to investigate the nature of the work beforehand. It is very important for people to speak to practitioners and work in paraprofessional or other capacities at least for a short time before committing themselves to an occupation.

The National Council on Rehabilitation Education surveys rehabilitation programs in colleges and universities every couple of years. According to its fact sheet for 1983–84, by Dick Ugland, Darryl Coffey, and Fred Menz, virtually all who completed a graduate program in rehabilitation went to work in the field. The number of graduates declined compared to the previous two-year period, perhaps because of fears that federal support for students in these programs would be cut—a fear that did not materialize. Federal aid is still generally available for graduate study in rehabilitation, and many schools have affirmative recruitment policies.

About one-third of these graduates went to work in the private sector. In all likelihood, many of the recent graduates who went to work for public agencies will transfer to the private sector after gaining more experience, thus contributing to the apparently high turnover rate discussed above. The report also found that 75 percent of the graduates of undergraduate programs in rehabilitation services were working in the field, an extremely high percentage.

SALARY, OTHER BENEFITS, AND WORKING CONDITIONS

Annual salaries in the private sector are in the $22,000 to $45,000 range, with top salaries of $90,000 possible. The hourly rate of compensation for a counselor in private practice is $55 to $65.

Beginning salaries in state agencies averaged $16,126 in 1984, the latest year for which data are available. The average salary in state agencies for experienced counselors was $25,650, but the range was very wide, going from $11,460 to $55,260. Department of Veterans Affairs counselors are classified as GS-12, which paid $34,580 to $44,957 in 1989.

Fringe benefits enjoyed by counselors depend on their employer. Counselors with state agencies and most private companies enjoy the usual benefits, such as paid vacations, health insurance, and pension plans. Private agencies may also provide an automobile for counselors.

Rehabilitation counselors perform most of their duties in regular offices. They must also visit employers, however, both to arrange placements and to follow up on the placement of clients.

ENTRY REQUIREMENTS AND CAREER LADDER

States show some variety in hiring requirements. Most agencies require either a bachelor's degree and two years of experience or a master's degree in rehabilitation counseling and no experience. Almost 30 percent of all state agencies, however, hire inexperienced holders of bachelor's degrees, while some other agencies require that even master's degree holders have work experience.

Private companies have the same hiring standards as state agencies, which is to say that holders of a master's degree in rehabilitation counseling are preferred but that other people are also sometimes hired. Increasingly, however, employers seek certified counselors.

A degree in rehabilitation counseling includes courses on the principles of rehabilitation, the psychosocial effects of disability, counseling techniques, and assessment. There are about eighty graduate programs for rehabilitation counseling and around fifteen undergraduate programs in rehabilitation services; most are either separate departments or part of a counselor education department in a school of education. More than seventy programs are accredited by the Council on Rehabilitation Education; about twice as many exist altogether.

The large number of rehabilitation counselors who have been certified—12,700 by January 1989—indicates its desirability. Certification of counselors is granted by the Board for Rehabilitation Certification, 1156 Shure Drive, Arlington Heights, Illinois 60004; (312) 394-2104. Two kinds of certificates are offered: certified rehabilitation counselor and certified insurance rehabilitation specialist. Several different categories of eligibility exist. A master's degree in rehabilitation counseling granted by a program accredited by the Council on Rehabilitation Education and completion of a six-hundred-hour internship supervised by a certified rehabilitation counselor qualifies an individual in one category, while other categories require one to seven years of work experience, depending on the kind of education a person has. The Board can provide specific information.

Advancement for counselors is usually a matter of promotion within the same agency or company. In fact, most state agencies do not hire above the entry level, preferring to promote from within. Some hiring at the mid-level does take place among private companies. Advancement may mean increased specialization in a particular aspect of rehabilitation, concentration on a particular form of disability, or increased administrative duties.

For more information about this occupation, contact state agencies that employ rehabilitation counselors. Among the directories that can be used to find individual counselors to speak to concerning the occupation are local guides to social and welfare service agencies and lists of registered counselors. The heading "rehabilitation services" is used in the classified telephone directory. Other relevant guides are listed in appendix B.

CHAPTER 10

COLLEGE COUNSELORS AND STUDENT AFFAIRS ADMINISTRATORS: FACTS AND FIGURES

OTHER JOB TITLES

Staff counselor, career counselor, crisis center coordinator, human development counselor, dean of students, vice-president for student affairs, vice-chancellor for academic affairs, director of student housing, director of alumni affairs, director of student counseling and placement, director of residence life, residence hall counselor, director of religious activities, student union director, foreign student advisor, veterans coordinator, student health services director, student organization advisor, advisor to fraternities and sororities organizations, recreation specialist, athletic director, financial aid administrator, director of admissions, registrar.

GOALS AND DUTIES

Assist all students in identifying and reaching their academic, personal, and vocational goals.

The difficulty with describing the work of high school counselors is that the single job title covers so many duties. The difficulty with college positions is quite the opposite; as the list above shows, postsecondary schools often use specialized titles and have separate departments for each of the services provided by guidance and counseling offices in high schools. In other cases, however, a person will wear several hats; for example, the financial aid administrator will also be the registrar, dean of students, or admissions officer.

The following services frequently come under the heading of student affairs:

- Academic counseling
- Financial aid counseling and administration
- Health services administration and counseling
- Coordination of student activities, including athletics
- Facilities management
- Vocational/career assessment and counseling
- Placement services
- Psychological counseling

A survey of chief student affairs officers conducted by Daniel Robinson for the National Association of Student Personnel Administrators in the 1987–88 academic year found that more than 80 percent of them were responsible for the counseling center, housing, career planning and placement, student health, student life, and the student union (a building in which extracurricular activities are held). Twenty percent were even responsible for security.

Each service involves a constellation of activities. For example, workers in a career planning and placement center may schedule interviews, distribute employment information, maintain a career and employer library, administer aptitude tests, run workshops on job-finding skills, cultivate contacts with potential employers, and, in addition to providing career counseling, perform academic counseling.

Some of these activities may seem remote from counseling, but the separation is often more apparent than real. Housing, for example, may include the training of resident advisors, who act as a first link in a counseling chain. Other activities—those related to a university counseling center, for example—are more obviously counseling activities. Furthermore, people in administrative positions often have additional duties involving counseling; for example, almost all of the career planning and placement directors who responded to a College Placement Council survey in December 1987 said that they performed personal counseling in addition to their career planning and placement activities. In fact, however, many postsecondary positions do require organizational and administrative skills as well as counseling skills.

Surveys of counselors in particular (rather than student affairs workers in general) have found that they spend the majority of their time on educational counseling and advisement. Other activities included conferring with students on probation, developing informative material on counseling-related topics, and planning orientation programs for new students. Providing services for students who intend to transfer was a significant activity for counselors in community colleges; these services include seminars, group meetings, campus visits, and college days. Counselors were assigned to veterans offices, handicapped programs, women's centers, career counseling centers, and financial aid offices where they might be responsible for the placement of students in work study programs as well as in the administration of loans and scholarships.

A 1985 survey of community college counselors in New Jersey found that they spent 64 percent of their time on individual or personal counseling and advisement; 15 percent of their time was taken up with administrative duties; and the rest of their time was divided among such activities as committee work, testing, group advising, teaching, and research.

EMPLOYMENT AND OUTLOOK

What cannot be defined can hardly be counted. The number of workers in student affairs depends on which occupations are included in the group. Registrars, for example, are certainly not counselors, although they do work in student affairs. Variation in size among institutions contributes to the uncertainty. At a very small school, a single person might administer both admissions and financial aid programs while a large school could have a dozen professionals in the placement office alone. The average counseling center in a community college employs two professional counselors.

Although precise employment data are unavailable, the following numbers will give a rough indication of the size of these occupations. The number of postsecondary institutions gives a fixed point of departure; according to the U.S. Department of Education, there are 5,669 public and private universities, colleges, and two-year institutions. Almost all have a placement office and other student affairs workers with some of the job titles listed. On large campuses, the director of student affairs may supervise fifty to a hundred professionals. Employment of fifty-five thousand or so is probable, according to several people in the field. Employment for particular specialties, according to the College and University Personnel Association, is given in the following tabulation of median salaries; these employment figures are almost certainly too low, however, because only the director is generally counted. For example, while only sixteen hundred people are listed for financial aid administration, the actual number of professionals working in financial aid could easily be double or triple the figure, according to a survey conducted by the National Association of Student Financial Affairs Administrators.

Despite the absence of a firm employment count, there is surprising agreement on the outlook for student affairs professionals: because employment is tied to enrollment and no growth in enrollment is expected, employment should remain stable. The U.S. Department of Education actually projects declines in college enrollment through 1997; although these projections are based on the sharp fall in the college-age population that is now occurring, it should be noted that enrollment has so far changed very little. At any rate, there will be numerous openings in order to replace workers who leave these occupations. People who work in educational programs that prepare these workers say that new graduates are still having some trouble finding jobs they desire, but the situation has improved somewhat over the past few years; entry-level jobs in residence hall administration have been especially numerous compared to the number of applicants for these positions.

SALARY, OTHER BENEFITS, AND WORKING CONDITIONS

Salary information for many of these jobs is collected by the College and University Personnel Association. The following figures come from its 1988–89 report.

Position Title	Median Salary	Number
Chief, student affairs	$50,256	1,096
Registrar	35,400	945
Chief facilities manager	42,432	1,001
Director, foreign students	31,400	207
Director, student financial aid	34,032	1,067
Associate director, student financial aid	25,920	504
Director, student placement	32,404	753
Director, student counseling	38,100	705
Associate director, student counseling	31,128	152
Director, student housing	30,625	542
Associate director, student housing	26,617	190
Housing officer, residence life	24,000	239

As always, the median salaries listed fail to show the considerable variation found in each occupation. For example, the survey conducted by the National Association of Student Personnel Administrators in the 1987–88 academic year found mean salaries similar to those given above but also revealed very wide ranges:

Position Title	Median Salary	Range
Chief student affairs officer	$53,000	$17,000 to $99,998
Officer for counseling	36,000	5,000 to 75,920
Officer for career planning and placement	32,000	6,000 to 63,444

Another example: the salaries of career counselors in December 1987, for example, ranged from under $15,000 to more than $50,000, according to the College Placement Council. The size of the school and whether it is privately run or publicly supported generally affect salaries a good deal—generally, but not always.

Student affairs workers enjoy the usual fringe benefits of college and university employees, including health insurance and pension programs. In many cases, they also pay reduced tuition rates and have the use of school recreational facilities. The cost of attending workshops, meetings, or conventions is also paid by the school in many cases. The physical working conditions are usually pleasant.

ENTRY REQUIREMENTS AND CAREER LADDER

Educational requirements vary somewhat from position to position. In general, a master's degree in student personnel and an internship served in a postsecondary institution is the minimum required; applicants with doctorates are preferred. According to the National Association of Student Personnel Administrators' 1987–88 survey, more than 60 percent of chief student affairs officers and officers for counseling held doctorates; by contrast, the highest degree for the officer for student financial aid was a bachelor's degree in 23 percent of the cases. Positions at smaller schools are frequently held by graduates of the institution; one-fifth of the financial aid administrators in 1977, for example, had attended the schools where they worked. Furthermore, surveys of people in student affairs often turn up a variety of educational backgrounds. For example, while the most common academic specialty for career planning and placement directors surveyed by the College Placement Council in 1987 was guidance and counseling, directors also had degrees in education, business administration, student personnel, higher education administration, education administration, counseling psychology, English, and psychology.

Among the titles for graduate programs that prepare these workers besides student personnel are college student development, student personnel services, community college counseling, community college management, community college leadership, student development in higher education, counseling and student personnel, college student personnel administration, and pupil and student personnel services. These programs are usually housed in a department of counselor education in a school of education. Between seventy to ninety programs are available nationwide.

People hired for counseling positions often need a doctorate in counseling, counseling psychology, or clinical psychology. One survey of campus counseling centers found that 65 percent of the directors had doctorates. About half the professionals on their staffs were licensed; these were evenly divided between psychologists and counselors.

The direction most people's careers will take becomes apparent while they are graduate students. Typically they will begin to focus on a specialty, such as financial aid or placement, and serve their practicum or internship in that field. A person's experience before earning a graduate degree may also affect his or her career; for example, nonacademic work experience is an invaluable asset to career counselors, according to the College Placement Council. Transfers from one specialty to another are made by people at various stages of their career, however. Note that teaching experience is not usually needed either for initial employment or advancement, although many people in student affairs do teach.

Advancement in these occupations can occur by moving up the administrative ladder within an institution or by moving from smaller to larger institutions. A doctorate may be required for advancement. The lack of growth projected for postsecondary institutions in general indicates that in the future promotions may be even more difficult to obtain than entry-level jobs.

For more information about these occupations, speak to the people on campus who have them. Information is also available in the books and journals listed in appendix B. Among the associations whose members work in one of these occupations are the College Placement Council, National Association of Student Activity Advisers, National Association of Student Financial Aid Administrators, National Association of Student Personnel Administrators, and the American College

Personnel Association of the American Association for Counseling and Development; addresses and more information for each are given in appendix A. Jobs in these fields are advertised in the newsletters and journals of the associations and in the *Chronicle for Higher Education,* which carried some five thousand such ads between 1979 and 1982.

CHAPTER 11

EMPLOYMENT AND CAREER COUNSELORS: FACTS AND FIGURES

OTHER JOB TITLES

Vocational counselor, career development specialist, job counselor.

GOALS AND DUTIES

To assist clients in choosing and preparing for a career and in finding a suitable job.

The basic duties of an employment counselor are interviewing, testing, counseling, referral to other agencies, and placement. Clients can come from any age group or employment background, and the counselor's duties naturally vary somewhat depending on the client's needs. The services that will benefit a young, single, recently discharged veteran may be of little use to a middle-aged steel worker who has a family and a mortgage. State agencies provide specialized services for groups such as veterans, youth, women, recipients of Aid for Dependent Children, older workers, the disabled, rural residents, and the economically disadvantaged.

An employment counselor usually begins by interviewing the client in order to learn what skills, experience, and education the client can bring to an employer. The counselor may then determine that additional aptitude and interest tests are needed. The counselor reviews the results of these tests with the client and assists the client in identifying suitable occupations. The counselor may find that the client needs further education or training and then provide information on suitable programs and financial aid. Or the client may simply need help with job-seeking skills that can be developed in group sessions. The counselor may act as a leader for such a group or job club. In other cases, the client may need no more than a job referral or assistance with a résumé. No matter where the client starts in relation to the world of work, the ultimate goal of client and counselor is placement in a specific job. Counselors then conduct follow-up interviews with former clients and their employers in order to learn the success of the placement.

Besides working on the clearly vocational concerns described above, these counselors also seek to reduce the psychological impact of unemployment and help people survive while unemployed. This might entail referring clients to other agencies or individual and group counseling sessions on subjects such as stress management and living on a reduced income.

Employment counseling requires knowledge of the work world as well as interviewing and counseling skills. The success of the counselor's office or agency depends in part on the counselor's relations with employers.

EMPLOYMENT AND OUTLOOK

The number of employment counselors probably exceeds three thousand. Of these, about fifteen hundred are with state agencies and the rest with private companies or other agencies. However, precise employment figures for state agencies, once collected by the federal government, are no longer available, and the total given is at best an educated guess. In 1989, roughly nine hundred career counselors were certified by the National Board for Certified Counselors.

Most employment counselors work for agencies of the state government that are largely supported by federal funds. The agency is usually called the Job Service, but other titles include the Employment Service and the Employment Security Agency. Counselors with the Job Service may either counsel full time or spend half their time or more in such noncounseling activities as intake interviewing, taking orders for job banks, administering tests, certifying program applicants, or leading job-search workshops.

Most private employment agencies employ few if any of these types of counselors because they are primarily concerned with rapidly placing individuals in jobs for which they have proven experience and not with career exploration. Besides the Job Service, therefore, the most likely employers are community agencies. In some cases, counselors in private practice specialize in employment concerns. A small but growing source of jobs has been the movement by large corporations to provide outplacement counseling to fired workers, especially at the executive level. The counselor may work directly for the corporation or, more often, for a private firm that contracts with the large company to provide the outplacement services.

The employment of counselors in state agencies declined slowly throughout the 1970s and then plummeted in 1982–83 as approximately one-third of the positions with the Job Service were cut. Nationwide, employment is declining, often through attrition. This trend is not expected to change. But funding decisions, which were once made by Congress, are now local. The situation varies dramatically from state to state and even from city to city. It also changes every year, along with political conditions.

Employment probably will increase in the private sector, although employment will lag behind the need for these services. The number of new positions will probably be relatively small in terms of the economy as a whole. One possible source of employment growth in the private sector is with firms that, under contract, provide services similar to those once provided by the Job Service.

Another possible source of employment is as a career development specialist with a corporation or large government agency. The United Auto Workers' current contract with the Ford Motor Company sets aside money to pay for the career counseling of laid-off workers; a single development such as this can lead to an increase in the number of counselors in private practice who have duties similar to those of an employment counselor.

The potential for private sector employment for counselors in career development is subject to dispute within the business community. At least one corporation hires only counseling psychologists with a doctorate for its program. Another one expresses reluctance to consider hiring people with any graduate degree from counselor education programs—the term *counselor* is viewed negatively. Businesses generally prefer to hire people with a degree in human relations development, in part because businesses are concerned that people trained in counselor education programs would be more interested in counseling individuals than in program management, which would be their primary duty. Whatever the reasons, career development programs in corporations are frequently administered by individuals who entered the corporate world after receiving undergraduate degrees and working in the corporation's human resources department.

Counselors are being hired by corporations and agencies, however, especially if they can show an understanding of business as demonstrated in undergraduate course work or familiarity with business gained through an internship dealing with corporate issues and served in a corporate setting. These positions are most appealing to those with an entrepreneurial spirit since the counselor must constantly sell the organization on the value of the service.

SALARY, OTHER BENEFITS, AND WORKING CONDITIONS

Little salary data is available. Members of the National Employment Counselors Association earned an average of $20,000 to $29,000 in 1986–87. The current salaries of state employees are available from each state.

Employment counselors who work for the state enjoy the usual benefits of state employees. No information is available concerning career counselors in private practice or career development specialists in the private sector.

ENTRY REQUIREMENTS AND CAREER LADDER

With fifty agencies doing the hiring, there are fifty sets of entry requirements. In general, states seek people with a bachelor's degree in one of the behavioral sciences or with additional courses in counseling; relevant professional experience can usually be substituted for education. Usually, a person must pass an examination given by the state's civil service or merit hiring board. Many states hire college graduates as employment interviewers; counselors are then trained and chosen from among the interviewers already employed. In other cases, states hire counselor trainees to begin with. To be considered for a promotion, a trainee or an interviewer may need to attend a graduate school program or an agency training program for counselors.

Only a few counselor education programs have the kind of emphasis sought by private industry for career development specialists. According to someone associated with these programs, however, the challenge facing graduates is less in proving their qualifications than in uncovering the jobs, because no central clearinghouse advertises these positions. In fact, almost all graduates of that program do find positions in the private sector or with large government agencies, although these positions are relatively few in number.

Employment counselors can advance to administrative positions within their agencies.

More information about this occupation is available from the counselor at local Job Service offices; one should be listed in the "state-government" section of your telephone book. General information about employment with state and local governments—including salaries, fringe benefits, and hiring practices—is available in *Opportunities in State and Local Government Careers* by Neale Baxter (Lincolnwood, Ill.: VGM Career Horizons, 1985). The National Board for Certified Counselors (5999 Stevenson Avenue, Alexandria, Virginia 22304) offers certification in a career counseling specialty.

Top: Medical social workers help patients and their families cope with illnesses. (Rush-Presbyterian-St. Luke's Medical Center photo) *Bottom:* Counseling psychologists sometimes refer people to outside sources of assistance to help them deal with personal needs. (D. Walsh photo)

CHAPTER 12

OTHER COUNSELING AND COUNSELING-RELATED OCCUPATIONS

The duties of workers in many occupations are closely related to those of counselors. Indeed, in some cases, drawing a line between counseling and other occupations can be extremely difficult. Among these occupations are alcohol and substance abuse counselors, counseling psychologists, school psychologists, and psychiatrists. Social workers and members of the clergy also use counseling techniques. Counselor educators are professors in graduate school departments that train counselors. Many professionals in the human resources development departments of large corporations also perform duties similar to those of counselors, although they tend to have more administrative responsibilities.

ALCOHOL AND DRUG ABUSE COUNSELOR

People who recognize, or are forced to face, their dependency on alcohol or other drugs often enter programs that provide medical monitoring, structure, an introduction to Alcoholics Anonymous or a similar fellowship, and counseling. The counseling may be conducted by specialists in the field who are known by various titles, such as addiction counselor, alcoholism counselor, chemical dependency counselor, drug abuse counselor, and substance abuse counselor. The counselor's duties include evaluating the client's condition, conducting individual and group counseling sessions, and meeting with other staff members to develop an individualized treatment program for each client. Work settings include hospitals, treatment centers, government agencies, and private practice.

These counselors number twenty-four thousand or so, according to the National Association of Alcoholism and Drug Abuse Counselors. The need for such counselors is great, judging by the number of alcoholics (more than twenty million) and other chemically dependent people in the country; but relatively few people seek treatment. Demand is also held down by lack of funds; funding for treatment programs is harder to come by than are denunciations of drugs and drunk drivers.

One distinguishing characteristic of this occupation, as opposed to other counseling occupations, is the variety of routes to employment. Although most alcohol and substance abuse counselors have a bachelor's degree, employers may not require one, in part because suitable courses were rarely offered by colleges in the past. This situation has begun to change, and some two-year and four-year colleges and graduate schools now provide appropriate training. In the absence of a fixed educational requirement, employers seek to hire individuals who have a competency-based certification. Certification requires experience, which can be acquired as a counselor-in-training. Employers hiring counselors-in-training look for people who have good counseling skills and are knowledgeable about the substances being abused, the nature of alcoholism and addiction, and the resources available to a recovering individual.

Certification of these counselors is available through states and other jurisdictions; it is voluntary. No national certification board exists; however, the National Commission on Accreditation of Alcoholism and Drug Abuse Credentialing Bodies has set standards for the states to follow. The minimum standards for certification usually include at least two years of supervised work experience as an alcoholism or drug abuse counselor, two hundred to three hundred clock hours of training, a written test, and a case presentation. Dual certification for alcohol and other drugs requires three years of supervised experience and is becoming increasingly important. More than thirty credentialing bodies have accepted these standards.

No national salary data have been collected, but these counselors earn approximately $16,000 to $23,000 a year; these earnings are generally less than those of nurses or social workers. Counselors in publicly funded programs perceive themselves as low paid.

More information about these workers appears in "Treating Addictions" by Michael Stanton in the *Occupational Outlook Quarterly,* Winter 1988. You can learn the names of local counselors to talk to about the occupation by contacting one of the programs listed under "alcoholism" in the yellow pages. *Directory of Academic Institutions and Organizations: Drug, Alcohol, and Employment Assistant Program Educational Resources* is a comprehensive listing of training programs published by the National Institute on Drug Abuse, U.S. Department of Health and Human Services. Published in 1988, single copies of the bulletin are available free while the supply lasts from the National Clearing House on Alcoholism and Drug Abuse Information, P.O. Box 2345, Rockville, Maryland 20852, (301) 468-2600.

COUNSELING PSYCHOLOGIST

According to the American Psychological Association (APA), counseling psychologists "provide services to promote individual and group well-being and to prevent and remedy developmental, educational, vocational, social and/or emotional adjustment problems." Like other counselors, they usually work with clients considered normal rather than patients considered ill; they are qualified to work with the maladjusted, however.

Although precise figures are unavailable, employment probably exceeds six thousand; more than three thousand members of the APA state that they are employed full time as counseling psychologists. Only clinical psychology is more often identified as a specialty by APA members; clinical psychology, however, is mentioned almost four times as often. The major employment settings for counseling psychologists who belong to Division 17 of the APA are schools, counseling centers, and private practice. More than 40 percent have private practice as their secondary employment setting, while it is the primary setting for 15 percent; the growing importance of private practice is indicated by the finding that younger counseling psychologists are twice as likely as older ones to be engaged in private practice. Other employment settings are hospitals, community mental health centers, full-time consultation, and government agencies.

In recent years, between 300 and 450 doctorates a year were awarded in counseling psychology. Surveys of previous classes found fewer than ten of the new doctors being unemployed, indicating that the supply does not currently exceed the demand. Even a very slow rate of growth, coupled with normal turnover, would suffice to make employment opportunities for new graduates favorable in this occupation.

The average salary of licensed psychologists with a doctorate who provided direct human services was $47,000 in 1987; those with a master's degree earned $35,000, on average. Counseling psychologists enjoy the usual fringe benefits granted by their employer.

Fully qualified counseling psychologists have a doctorate in their field from a program accredited by the APA; there were fifty-one such programs in 1988. Use of the job title *psychologist* by people who are offering services to the public is controlled in every state. Common requirements, besides the doctorate, are one to two years of experience and successful performance on an examination. A list of these boards and their addresses is available from the APA, whose address is in appendix A.

More information about this occupation is available in *Opportunities in Psychology Careers* by Donald E. Super and Charles M. Super (Lincolnwood, Ill.: VGM Career Horizons, 1988) and in the other sources of information listed in the appendixes.

COUNSELOR EDUCATOR

Counselor educators instruct and train future counselors, usually in graduate school counselor education programs. Their duties and the degree of their specialization vary greatly, depending on the size and emphasis of the program with which they are associated. As university professors, they are responsible for designing courses, lecturing, assigning research projects, and evaluating the progress of students. Many conduct original research. They also supervise prospective counselors during practicums and internships. Counselor educators like Dr. Seligman, who is interviewed in an earlier chapter, often combine their professorial duties with a counseling practice, either in association with the school's counseling center or in private.

According to Joseph Hollis and Richard Wantz, there are 1,392 full-time counselor educators and about twice as many part-time ones. Universities are the major employers, of course. A counselor education program may have a single full-time faculty member and a couple of part-time teachers; large programs employ twenty or more instructors and professors.

The general outlook for college professors is very poor because of the projected decline in the number of eighteen- to twenty-five-year-olds, the group that traditionally has accounted for the majority of college students. This trend projection should be viewed with caution for two reasons. First, it is not necessarily relevant to the outlook for any particular teaching specialty. Because of the many different specialties of college teachers and the relatively small number of people in each, no particular outlook information is usually available. In the case of counselor educators, employment will rise if a favorable job market for counselors begins to attract large numbers of students to the field. Second, high school students considering this occupation will not be prepared to enter it until after the year 2000, by which time the number of eighteen-year-olds will have risen.

A Ph.D. in counseling or a related field is generally required for these positions. Among the specialties within the field are school, rehabilitation, and marriage and family therapy. Almost 90 percent of all counselor educators do in fact have doctorates. Those with only a master's degree are most likely to be part-time instructors or graduate students completing their doctoral programs.

In 1986-87, the average nine- or ten-month salary in student counseling and personnel services ranged from $22,602 for instructors to $40,472 for full professors in public senior colleges and universities and college and university teachers, according to one survey. According to the American Association of University Professors, average salaries in all fields in 1987–88 ranged from $22,190 for instructors to $47,220 for professors. Incidentally, between 1983–84 and 1987–88, faculties' salaries rose more rapidly than inflation. Besides the usual fringe benefits, professors may be granted sabbaticals by their schools in order to pursue research projects.

College teachers usually begin their careers as either instructors or assistant professors, later advancing to the ranks of associate and full professor. Advancement often hinges on publication or other evidence of a growing reputation in a person's field.

The American Association of University Professors, One Dupont Circle, Suite 500, Washington, D.C. 20036, can provide information about college and university teaching in general. The Association for Counselor Education and Supervision represents counselor educators within the American Association for Counseling and Development, 5999 Stevenson Avenue, Alexandria, Virginia 22304. Faculty members of counselor education programs—especially the largest ones—are the best sources of information about the nature of the work and the current and projected job market in this field.

MEMBER OF THE CLERGY

Many members of the clergy—ministers, priests, and rabbis—devote much of their time to counseling activities. About three thousand are members of the American Association of Pastoral Counselors, 9508A Lee Highway, Fairfax, Virginia 22031. Although counseling may become the primary duty of many clerics, they usually follow this vocation for other reasons. The decision to enter the clergy should be based on one's religious convictions. *Opportunities in Religious Service Careers,* by John Oliver Nelson (Lincolnwood, Ill.: VGM Career Horizons, 1988), discusses why a person should enter the clergy and offers practical advice to those interested in a religion-oriented career.

Some counselor education programs in universities have programs in pastoral counseling. Members of the clergy who wish to receive training in counseling can also contact the Association for Clinical Pastoral

Education, Inc., 1549 Clairmont Road, Suite 103, Decatur, Georgia 30033, (404) 320-1472. It accredits and publishes a directory of supervisors and training centers in hospitals, other health care institutions, and prisons.

PARAPROFESSIONAL

The term *paraprofessional* usually refers to a job that does not require a college degree. Medicine now employs many paraprofessionals in a variety of technical occupations. No comparable growth has occurred in counseling, where the term is used loosely of workers who take over some of the noncounseling functions in an office, such as updating a referral directory. Paraprofessionals in counseling are likely to have entered the field as clerical workers and then taken on more responsibility as they gained experience.

Rehabilitation has seen some growth in employment of people with less than a counselor's training. These individuals are usually college graduates, however, often having attended an undergraduate program in rehabilitation services. Although they may be referred to as paraprofessionals, they would be classified as professionals by most of the organizations that collect employment data.

PSYCHIATRIST

Psychiatrists are medical doctors who diagnose and treat mental illnesses. Although they may use counseling or psychological techniques, they may also prescribe drugs or electroshock therapy. They are the only mental health professionals authorized to prescribe drugs.

Psychiatrists may have a general practice or they may specialize in a field such as industrial psychiatry, forensic psychiatry, or psychoanalysis. Child psychiatry is considered a separate specialty by the American Medical Association.

Of the 430,000 medical doctors in America, about 32,000 are psychiatrists, according to the American Medical Association. About half have full-time private practices. In June 1986, the equivalent of 18,000 worked full-time in hospitals and other institutions serving the mentally ill, according to the National Institute of Mental Health. Administrating community mental health centers, teaching in medical school, and conducting research are among the duties of other psychiatrists, often in combination with a part-time private practice.

The average net earnings for psychiatrists was $86,670 in 1982, according to the American Medical Association. Although these earnings are much higher than those in other occupations, they are lower than the average net earnings of all physicians, which exceed $106,300 a year.

Psychiatrists must be licensed to practice medicine, which means that they must graduate from an accredited medical school and pass the appropriate examinations. Entrance into medical school is extremely competitive. Generally, psychiatrists spend four years in residency programs after medical school and then take exams administered by the American Board of Psychiatry and Neurology.

Physicians have enjoyed a very favorable job market for the past generation, at least in part because of the restrictions on the number of students in medical schools. In the future, physicians starting a practice are expected to face somewhat more competition than they have recently. Psychiatry, which is entered by so few medical school graduates, should be less competitive.

More information about this occupation is available in *Opportunities in Psychiatry* by Fenton Keyes (Lincolnwood, Ill.: VGM Career Horizons, 1982). The Office of Related Health Professions, American Medical Association, 535 North Dearborn Street, Chicago, Illinois 60610, (312) 645-5000, can also provide information. The Association of American Medical Colleges, Suite 301, 1776 Massachusetts Avenue, Washington, D.C. 20036, (202) 828-0400, can provide a list of approved medical schools and general information on premedical education, financial aid, and medicine as a profession.

PUPIL PERSONNEL WORKER

These professionals visit the homes of students who have not been attending school. They speak to the child's parents or guardians, seeking to learn the reason for the student's absence. Reasons can include fear of school, a lack of proper clothing or nutrition, or other problems. The pupil personnel worker seeks a solution, which can require referral to other agencies, such as the social services department. Counseling during the course of several visits may be necessary before the problem is resolved. If there are pockets of truancy within a building or neighborhood, the pupil personnel worker may contact other agencies of the government, such as the recreation department, to set up tutorial or other educational programs outside the school. Other job titles for these workers are attendance workers, truant officers, and visiting teachers.

Employment figures for this occupation are not collected. Employment could easily exceed ten thousand, however, since one worker would be needed for every two thousand to four thousand students. Detailed salary information is not available either. Salaries for these workers are certainly somewhat higher than those of teachers, however, and are often supplemented by a travel allowance. Employment is usually year round.

These are not entry-level positions. The typical pupil personnel worker has several years experience within a school system as a teacher, administrator, or counselor in addition to specialized training, such as a master's degree in guidance. Recruitment is usually conducted within the school system. All states certify these workers. Although there is an International Association of Pupil Personnel Workers, the best sources of additional information about this occupation are the state departments of education—listed in appendix C—and local school districts.

SCHOOL PSYCHOLOGIST

School psychologists, like school counselors, work to improve the intellectual, social, and emotional development of children. According to the National Association of School Psychologists, Inc., school psychology "focuses upon the psycho-educational development of individuals, their abilities and potentialities, and the emotional and cultural factors which influence this learning process."

As with other occupations, their duties vary with the employer. In some school districts they practically function as elementary school counselors, providing counseling and consultation services to the students and teachers in two or three schools. In others, school psychologists might work almost exclusively as counselors for students with adjustment problems or with families undergoing unusual stress. In yet another, school psychologists will be actively engaged in curriculum development or in-service training.

School psychologists, being responsible for the placement of students in programs that will be most beneficial, often have a special concern with assessment. Assessment is based on a psycho-educational evaluation of the student's personal social adjustment, intelligence, academic achievement, sensory and perceptual motor functioning, and environmental or cultural influences. On average, school psychologists spend 40 percent of their time on assessment and the rest on intervention, which includes counseling and other duties.

Total employment exceeds twenty thousand. Federal law mandates that states allocate funds for the employment of one school psychologist for every two thousand students. Current employment approaches that goal, according to several studies. Little growth is expected. However, even slight growth coupled with normal turnover will result in fifteen hundred openings per year. In 1985–86, 1,552 master's degrees were awarded in school psychology, according to the U.S. Department of Education. This would indicate a balance between supply and demand, but experts say that current demand has exploded and that the supply of school psychologists is too small. Shortages exist in medium-size cities as well as in large urban and small rural districts. The recognition of this situation by one school board in 1988 caused it to use Federal Express to send its job announcements to graduate schools. In other words, the job market is good now and expected to get even better.

Comprehensive salary data is not collected for this occupation. A survey of its members by the National Association of School Psychologists found that 50 percent of the respondents were earning between $22,000 and $34,000 a year in December 1986; salaries lower than $13,000 and higher than $52,000 were also reported. Other sources indicate that psychologists with a doctorate who work in elementary and high school settings earned about $45,000 in 1987, on average.

A fully qualified school psychologist has a master's degree plus about seventy-two graduate school credits in school psychology as well as supervised experience in the field. Such an education program leads to an educational specialist degree, which requires roughly twice the number of credits that a master's degree does. Doctorate programs are also available. In recent years, the number of students proceeding to a doctorate has increased, in part because of the status of the doctorate as the entry-level degree for other psychology specialties; 505 doctorate degrees were awarded in school psychology in 1985–86, according to the U.S. Department of Education. Master's and doctorate programs are accredited by the National Council for the Accreditation of Teacher Education, 1919 Pennsylvania Avenue, NW, Suite 202, Washington, D.C. 20006, (202) 466-7496. It publishes a list of programs annually. School psychologists must be certified by their state's department of education or department of public instruction (addresses are listed in appendix C). Certification as a school psychologist is not a license to practice psychology.

More information about this occupation is available from the National Association of School Psychologists, Inc., Suite 200, 808 Seventeenth Street, NW, Washington, D.C. 20006, (202) 223-9498. It currently has fifteen thousand members. Information also appears in *Opportunities in Psychology Careers* by Donald E. Super and Charles M. Super (Lincolnwood, Ill.: VGM Career Horizons, 1988) and the other sources of information listed in the appendixes.

SOCIAL WORKER

Social workers—who are much more numerous than counselors—provide counseling for individuals, families, and groups. Among their other duties are the administration of aid programs and the referral of clients to other agencies for some services, such as job training or day care. The speedy identification of a client's needs and the implementation of a plan to supply essential food, shelter, clothing, and medical attention probably account for more of the average social worker's time than does counseling. Individual social workers, however, may be primarily concerned with counseling.

Social workers may specialize in particular fields. About half of all social workers are in just three categories: mental health, child/youth, and medical/health. Those working in mental health frequently work in a community mental health clinic or outpatient psychiatric clinic, helping patients adjust to their conditions. Child welfare workers counsel children; advise and consult with parents, teachers, and others; arrange for homemaker services; and start legal action to protect neglected or abused children. Medical social workers help patients and their families plan for discharges and work to coordinate the services of the many different agencies that provide help to people in need.

Social workers usually have an eight-hour day, five days a week. Part of their time is spent in comfortable offices, but they must also visit clients.

The usual educational requirement is a bachelor's degree in social work, psychology, or sociology. A bachelor's degree in social work includes courses in human behavior, social work methods, social welfare policies, and supervised field experience. Some positions require a master of social work degree.

More than forty states require that social workers be licensed or registered.

Salaries for social workers ranged from $16,700 to $31,000 a year in 1985. They vary widely by setting, experience, and duties. Social workers receive the usual fringe benefits.

About 365,000 people worked as social workers in 1986. The major employers are departments of human resources, social services, mental health, housing, education, and correction. Many private organizations also provide social services and employ social workers, including community service organizations, religious communities, and large corporations. Furthermore, social workers, like counselors, are increasingly entering private practice.

The number of social workers is rising faster than the average for all occupations. Many positions will become available because of turnover, which is relatively high for this occupation. The needs of a growing and aging population will also increase the demand for workers in this field.

More information about this occupation is available from the following associations.

National Association of Social Workers
7981 Eastern Avenue
Silver Spring, MD 20910
Council on Social Work Education
1744 R Street, NW
Washington, DC 20009.

Information also appears in *Opportunities in Social Work Careers* by Renee Wittenberg (Lincolnwood, Ill.: VGM Career Horizons, 1988). General information about employment with state and local governments—including salaries, fringe benefits, and hiring practices—is available in *Opportunities in State and Local Government Careers* by Neale Baxter (Lincolnwood, Ill.: VGM Career Horizons, 1985).

Important characteristics for a counselor include concern for individuals, empathy, emotional stability, patience, objectivity, and a sense of humor. (Ball State University photo)

CHAPTER 13

CHARACTERISTICS OF A COUNSELOR

Can I see another's woe/ And not be in sorrow too?
Can I see another's grief/ And not seek for kind relief?
—William Blake

WHAT MAKES A GOOD COUNSELOR?

When describing the characteristics of counselors, some writers sound almost as though they are talking about Claire and Cliff Huxtable, the parents on "The Cosby Show." The combination of concern for individuals, empathy, emotional stability, patience, objectivity, and sense of humor that they demonstrate is mentioned again and again.

Empathy usually leads the list. By empathy, writers mean more than sympathy. They mean that the counselor doesn't just feel sorry for the client but can actually identify with the client, can take a hike in the client's Reebok's. Empathy implies other important characteristics. For example, a counselor must be broadminded, sensitive to others, tolerant, and understanding, recognizing people's right to be different. Without these qualities, counselors cannot work effectively with a range of clients. C. Gilbert Wrenn, the respected author of *The World of the Contemporary Counselor,* alludes to these important qualities when he writes, "I have begun to think that the ability to listen with understanding, and without apparent threat to either counselor or client, is a most important attribute of an effective counselor."

Empathy is not enough, of course. Counseling is an alternating current. Not only must a counselor identify with a client, the client must recognize the counselor's concern. Successful counselors are friendly, pleasant, and tactful. They like people—seeing others as able, dependable, and worthy—and people like counselors. They are sincere, and people recognize their sincerity. They are trustworthy, and people see them as such.

Counselors cannot wallow in a sea of emotion, however, or confuse the client's success with their own. Although empathy is essential in both identifying the client's problems and winning the client's trust, objectivity is needed to find solutions. Solutions also require a thorough knowledge of possibilities and respect for facts. Typical counselors, therefore, would score well on both the verbal and mathematical components of aptitude tests. They are alert and can communicate clearly with all sorts of people.

Besides understanding others, counselors must understand themselves. They must recognize their own strengths and accept their own weaknesses. Their sense of humor goes hand in hand with self-knowledge, for it helps keep them levelheaded and tolerant of ambiguity. It goes without saying that their sense of humor is directed at themselves and not—ever—at a client.

The preceding paragraphs describe a counselor's characteristics. A slightly different way to show what an occupation requires is to discuss the skills needed. If the primary characteristic of counselors is empathy, their primary skill is interviewing. It is interviewing skills that enable them to move from testing and providing information to counseling individuals or leading groups.

DOWNERS AND UPPERS

Every silver lining has a cloud, and every occupation has its drawbacks. Satisfaction for a worker occurs only when the positive features of the profession outweigh the downers. Counseling has its share of negative attributes.

Characteristics of a Counselor 79

Counselors are subject to adverse criticism, some of it contradictory. One group will claim that counseling is an inefficient waste of money while another complains that counselors spend too much time playing games with "interesting" problems and not enough on the average client. A counselor who works for a program supported by tax money—as most do—is especially vulnerable to attacks of inefficiency, because the attack can affect both self-esteem and funding, resulting in poorer performance.

Besides general criticism, counselors are also subject to second guessing by parents, other relatives, and friends of the client. No matter how unfounded, such criticism is not likely to be pleasant. In order to be satisfied with this occupation, a person must be able to shrug off such criticism or—better—to find in it suggestions for improvement.

Yet another downer is that no counselor can be successful with every client. Students turn away from their future, people remain unemployed, alcoholics relapse, families break apart despite the best effort of the counselor. Accepting such failures is probably a counselor's most difficult task.

Less pressing negative aspects of the occupation have already been alluded to. Counseling is not a way to great wealth or high prestige. These are minor complaints for most practicing counselors, who, typically, are more concerned about administrative pressures and a lack of time to counsel than they are about their salary.

What does the satisfied counselor balance against these downers? The client's success. Counselors who enjoy their work like working closely with others and showing them how to achieve their goals. Simply engaging in this kind of activity is rewarding to them. The greatest reward, however, is when the client uses the tools provided by the counselor to actually reach the goal set. Not that the counselor can take credit for the client's work, of course. Just as a good Little League coach never claims victory when the team wins, counselors do not confuse their efforts with the client's. Still, counselors do feel great satisfaction when a course of action they have taken with a client pays off in greater success for that client.

No one has all the attributes of a successful, satisfied counselor in full measure. You will probably be most satisfied as a counselor, however, if you have a deep desire to help others along with the willingness and ability to do the hard work required to learn how to help.

CHAPTER 14

EDUCATION FOR COUNSELORS

There are some things which cannot be learned quickly, and time, which is all we have, must be paid heavily for their acquiring.
—Ernest Hemingway

Effective counseling in our complicated world requires more than the personality characteristics described in the last chapter. It also requires a solid academic background. Except for alcohol and drug abuse counselors, whose special entry requirements are described with the other information on that occupation, most positions for counselors require at least a master's degree; earning one usually takes at least one year of full-time study after college. Accredited Ph.D. programs require at least three years of full-time study and an additional year of supervised experience. Students must begin their educational planning in high school to make sure that they will qualify for college.

In college, prospective counselors have four possible options; they might, however, be restricted to a single academic major, depending on their state's regulations governing certification in the specialty they plan to enter. If the student's only concern is admission to graduate school, any academic major will do in most cases since counselor education programs in graduate schools usually accept students without regard to major, although many programs require applicants to have three to five undergraduate courses in psychology or another behavioral science. A second option—the one usually recommended—is to major in psychology or another behavioral science. A third possibility for undergraduates is to major in counselor education. About seventy colleges and universities have such a program, and about thirty offer a bachelor's degree in rehabilitation services administration. This option may be especially attractive to people planning to enter rehabilitation counseling. An undergraduate major in rehabilitation services can shorten a person's stay in graduate school by a semester or more. Fourth, a student may need to major in education in order to qualify for a teaching position so that he or she can gain required teaching experience.

Because certification may be restricted to people with teaching experience, students should try to clarify their goals no later than their sophomore year in college. They must first determine the kind of counseling they wish to do. Entry positions in rehabilitation counseling, for example, are more likely to be available to qualified college graduates than positions as school counselors.

The chapters on facts and figures in this book present the usual entry requirements for various specialties. Students should, however, learn precise requirements from credentialing authorities. In particular, students may wish to learn if teaching experience is required of school counselors and if other states recognize the certificate for the student's specialty. The credentialing authorities are listed in appendix C.

Similarly, general employment requirements are given in this book, but students would do well to learn exact requirements of the employers they are most likely to work for. For example, many states hire entry-level rehabilitation counselors with a bachelor's degree and no experience, but Iowa does not. A state may not require that school counselors have teaching experience, but a local school district might. Also remember that no matter what education is required for entry, additional education may be required for advancement.

Graduate schools can provide information on entry requirements for their programs. Should a school call for certain undergraduate courses, for example, you'll be able to take them before graduation. Entry requirements vary widely by program. On average, master's programs require scores on the Graduate Record Exam (GRE), of at least 459 on the verbal and 455 on the quantitative section. Alternatively, a minimum score of 40 on the Miller Analogy Test may be required. From three to five courses in psychology or counseling are also required by many programs. Other typical requirements are a 2.7 undergraduate grade point average (based on straight A's equalling 4.0), letters of recommendation, personal interviews, and relevant work experience. Requirements for doctoral programs are somewhat higher than those for master's programs.

PICKING A PROGRAM

Almost five hundred institutions offer more than one thousand different programs to prepare counselors. Most programs—even those in counseling psychology, rehabilitation counseling, or mental health counseling—are housed in a school of education; programs are also housed in schools of arts and sciences, however. Programs for different kinds of counselors may be in different departments within a school or institution.

The educational choice, in other words, is wide. You will want to consider many different factors before selecting the schools you wish to apply to. The following are some points to bear in mind:

- Accreditation
- Client emphasis
- Philosophical orientation
- Counseling specialties offered
- Nature and extent of field experience
- Degree requirements
- Correlation of degree requirements with certification requirements
- Degree granted
- Entry requirements
- Location
- Size
- Faculty-student ratio
- Location of field experience
- Placement of recent graduates
- Cost
- Availability of scholarships and loans

Whether or not a program is accredited may be particularly important. As recently as ten years ago, no programs were accredited specifically for counseling. Now, many are. But the situation continues to change rapidly. You should be especially careful in evaluating programs that are not accredited and have no plans to seek accreditation.

Numerous general directories of colleges and graduate schools are available; several are listed in appendix B.

Counselor Preparation, 1986–89: Programs, Personnel, Trends, by Joseph W. Hollis and Richard A. Wantz, is the sixth edition of the most complete specialized directory of programs in counselor preparation published. In addition to a discussion of trends in counselor education, the book includes detailed descriptions of hundreds of programs. Each description gives a complete list of the faculty, degree(s) awarded, number of male and female graduates in each program per year, credit hour and practicum hour requirements, accreditation, percentage of students receiving financial aid, setting of experiential components, placement setting of graduates, courses recently added, and a statement by the school on the unique features of the program. New editions appear every three years. The publisher is Accelerated Development, Muncie, Indiana 47304, (317) 284-7511.

The accreditation boards for different types of programs publish lists of accredited programs. National boards include the following.

Council for Accreditation of Counseling and Related Educational Programs (CACREP)
5999 Stevenson Avenue
Alexandria, Virginia 22304
(703) 823-9800

CACREP accredits master's degree programs in four areas: community counseling, mental health counseling, school counseling, and student affairs practice in higher education. It also accredits doctoral programs in counselor education and supervision. In February 1989, fifty-one programs were accredited. People in counselor education expect that only graduates of accredited programs will be considered for many job openings once a substantial number of schools has been accredited.

American Psychological Association (APA)
Accreditation for Counseling Psychology Programs
1200 17th Street, NW
Washington, D.C. 20036
(202) 955-7600

The APA currently accredits fifty-one doctoral programs in counseling psychology. A directory of all accredited programs in psychology, called *Graduate Study in Psychology,* is published annually. The Association also publishes lists of programs three times a year in its journal, *American Psychologist.*

Council on Rehabilitation Education, Inc. (CORE)
185 North Wabash Avenue
Room 1617
Chicago, Illinois 60601
(312) 346-6027

CORE accredits graduate programs in rehabilitation counseling; sixty-nine programs are currently approved, and five programs have received preliminary approval.

Commission on Accreditation for Marriage and Family Therapy Education
1717 K Street, NW, Suite 407
Washington, D.C. 20006
(202) 429-1825

An arm of the American Association for Marriage and Family Therapy, the Commission accredits diploma, master's, doctoral, and certification programs; forty-one programs are currently accredited. As of January 1989, two sets of standards were in use, resulting in differences between accredited programs. Only one standard will be in use by 1993.

National Council for the Accreditation of Teacher Education
1750 Pennsylvania Avenue, NW, Room 411
Washington, D.C. 20006
(202) 466-7496

This organization accredits schools of education; as a minimum, a counselor education program should be housed in a school of education accredited by this board.

Association for Clinical Pastoral Education, Inc.
1549 Clairmont Road, Suite 103
Decatur, Georgia 30033
(404) 320-1472

An interfaith organization, the Association accredits training programs for members of the clergy who perform counseling. It publishes a directory of training centers, seminaries, and supervisors.

WHAT DO YOU LEARN?

Almost any counselor education program is likely to include course work on career development theory, the use of educational and vocational information, statistics, research methods, testing and measurement, counseling theory and technique, the organization and administration of services and the employment setting, psychological development and human behavior, group counseling procedures, and professional ethics. Supervised counseling experience is also provided through a laboratory, practicum, or internship. Internships follow a practicum and may last a full school year. They are usually set in schools or community agencies, such as rehabilitation agencies, mental health clinics, hospitals, marriage and family counseling centers, correctional institutions, diagnostic centers, or employment agencies. Employers often consider the appropriateness of the setting of the internship when comparing the merits of different applicants. For example, the likelihood of your being employed in the private sector is very much improved if you have performed an internship in such a setting.

In a previous edition of their directory, Hollis and Wantz classified the educational experiences offered in counselor education programs into eight categories, ranging from cognitive (traditional classroom procedures) to conjoint (the sharing of duties with a working professional). From their list, it is evident that all the following methods are used to educate counselors: readings, discussions, lectures, research projects, video recordings, films, observation of counseling sessions, role playing, field trips, internships, and work as a student counselor under supervision.

Differences among the programs for various specialties can appear at any point. For example, a program for secondary school counselors might require a course in adolescent psychology while the elementary school program specifies child psychology. Programs accredited by CACREP must require these core courses: human growth and development, social and cultural foundations, helping relationships, groups, life-style and career development, appraisal, research and evaluation, and professional orientation. CORE-accredited programs require courses on the principles and practice of rehabilitation counseling; medical aspects of disability; and utilizing community resources. The model curriculum proposed by the American Association for Marriage and Family Therapy requires two to four courses in each of the following three areas: marriage and family systems, marriage and family therapy, and individual development. The differences are greatest, however, in the particular internship, practicum, or supervised counseling that the student engages in.

The average practicum in a master's program lasts two hundred contact hours and the average internship three hundred to six hundred hours; both practicums and internships are twice as long in doctoral programs. The length of these experiences varies according to the student's specialty. Marriage and family therapy programs typically require more supervised experience and school or student affairs programs less. The Ed.D. programs also tend to require less supervised experience than the Ph.D. programs.

WHAT IS IT LIKE?

This chapter gives a rather dry rundown of requirements and course offerings. Counseling is not simply academic, however, and counselor education is not simply the mastery of information. Students in a counselor education program go through the emotions of fear, testing, discovery, and fuller realization of self.

TRENDS TO KEEP TRACK OF

Current issues in counseling are discussed in a subsequent chapter. Some of them are directly related to counselor education, however. In particular, the number of credit hours required in accredited programs is greater than the requirements of traditional master's degree programs in most fields. Roughly thirty-six semester hours are required in most programs, but accredited counselor-preparation programs require forty-eight. The amount of time spent in supervised counseling is also greater than was required in most programs before the accreditation movement got underway. Nevertheless, accredited programs attract more applicants.

Another change affecting education is the increasing specialization of counselors. Not so long ago, almost all programs were designed for school counselors with a few courses on subjects such as marriage and family counseling or rehabilitation counseling offered as electives. Now, however, programs designed specifically for agency counseling, pastoral counseling, and all the other counseling specialties are becoming common. Recently, schools have been adding courses in marriage and family, geriatric, substance abuse, legal, and ethical issues. According to Hollis and Wantz, programs for marriage and family counseling/therapy have been increasing in number while the number of programs for school and rehabilitation counselors has remained stable over the past few years.

CHAPTER 15

COUNSELING'S PAST

The best of prophets of the future is the past.
—George Gordon, Lord Byron

Counseling is an American occupation that grew out of the country's promise to its citizens. The late 1800s, a period of gross materialism and blatant political corruption, are sometimes called the Gilded Age. Gilding is even less than skin deep, however, and underneath the glitter of millionaires, debutantes, and mansions in this period and the following decades was the reality of the muckrakers and social reformers such as Ida Tarbell and Jacob Riis. Waves of immigrants from Europe and migrants from American farms were flooding the cities. The newcomers looked for hope and opportunity but found disease and destitution. The country was not ready to accept such conditions, however. A series of reform movements providing for settlement houses, improved sanitation, better housing, and access to education helped relieve some of the worst conditions. One of those movements led to the counseling profession that exists today.

EARLY PROGRAMS

Guidance, as counseling was called until recently, had no founder. It is too multifaceted an activity for that. But one person, Frank Parsons, is often called its father; he established the Vocational Bureau in Boston in 1908. Even earlier, George Merril had started a vocational guidance program in San Francisco, and Jessie B. Davis, in Detroit, had devoted classroom time to guidance activities. In 1907, as principal of Central High in Grand Rapids, Michigan, Davis made character development and vocational information part of the curriculum. At this same period, similar programs began in Cincinnati, Chicago, De Kalb (Illinois), Denver, Lincoln (Nebraska), Los Angeles, Minneapolis, New York City, Oakland, Omaha, Providence (Rhode Island), Salt Lake City, and Seattle. Even earlier, books such as *The Book of Trades* or *Library of Useful Arts* had appeared to help people learn about occupations.

The early programs all focused on vocational information, but they were also concerned with discovering how to match individuals with the occupations that would suit them best so that they could fully develop their potential. Parsons, in particular, is credited with making such matching a systematic activity. In *Choosing a Vocation,* he writes that a person must take three steps before selecting a field of work: First, develop a clear understanding of yourself—your aptitudes, abilities, interests, resources, limitations, and other qualities. Second, gain a knowledge of the requirements and conditions of success, advantages and disadvantages, compensations, opportunities, and prospects in different lines of work. Third, achieve true reasoning on the relation of these two groups of facts.

PROGRESS IN COUNSELING

The years that followed saw rapid progress. Counselors organized the National Vocational Guidance Association in 1913. Other organizations followed, many of which merged to form the American Personnel and Guidance Association in 1952. It became the American Association for Counseling and Development in 1984.

Development of Tests

The work of Sigmund Freud, Carl Jung, and Clifford Beers—who launched the mental hygiene movement—fueled improvements in the treatment of mental illness and initiated programs to identify mental illness early. The development of the intelligence test by Alfred Binet led to great interest in testing and measurement on the part of the army as well as educators. World War I brought about mass testing of individuals for the first time. Improvements in the validity of various tests were made, and even more extensive testing occurred during World War II.

Carl Rogers

Besides testing, the 1940s are important for the publication of *Counseling and Psychotherapy* by Carl Rogers. Rogers stressed the importance of the counseling relationship; his work thus acted as a counterweight to the diagnostic/testing developments of the war. The importance of the clients' or students' own perceptions of their needs was reemphasized.

Government Support

The Great Depression and World War II increased the federal government's support for guidance activity in many ways. This support included funds for research on vocations and training programs for counselors as well as the employment of counselors. The government encouraged counseling in a great many areas; veterans, the unemployed, and elementary schoolchildren were added to those with access to counselors. The National Defense Education Act of 1958 was especially significant in regard to federal involvement in counseling. One writer, Verne Faust, points to passage of this law as the "beginning of the modern elementary school counseling of any considerable dimension." Its impact is seen in the growing number of school counselors of all types. From 1958 to 1961 their numbers doubled, and the ratio of students to counselors fell dramatically.

The 1960s also saw significant changes in our society's approach to mental health. Successful attempts were made to reduce the number of patients in long-term hospitals. Many factors contributed to this reduction, including the discovery of new drugs that controlled the symptoms of some types of mental illness. Part of the change was also due to an increased emphasis on comprehensive care, which stressed preventive measures. Counselors played an important part in these programs.

Rehabilitation Services

Rehabilitation became a more important function of counselors after World War II, although earlier efforts had been made. More than 600,000 World War II veterans received rehabilitation services by the end of 1953. Over the years, the number of people eligible for rehabilitation services grew to include the physically disabled, emotionally handicapped, mentally retarded, and recovering substance abusers. The late 1970s saw the inclusion of rehabilitation as a mandatory part of worker's compensation in state laws, beginning with California. The employment of rehabilitation counselors in the private sector has increased significantly as other states have followed suit.

Corporations have also contributed to the growth of the counseling professions. Besides their obvious use of testing and job analysis, they have employed counselors to assist workers with a great many concerns ranging from alcoholism to retirement.

CHAPTER 16

COUNSELING'S PRESENT: APPROACHES AND TECHNIQUES

The ways counselors go about their duties are as varied as the counselors themselves. By and large, however, they make use of certain standard approaches and techniques.

CURRENT APPROACHES TO COUNSELING

In their description of counselor education programs, Joseph Hollis and Richard Wantz identify a dozen different approaches or primary practice orientations that counseling programs might have. An eclectic orientation, in which a counselor does not express a preference for one approach over another, allowing the conditions of the particular case to determine the approach, is the most common. Other common approaches include client centered, behavioral, and cognitive. These four orientations account for about 80 percent of all approaches. Other orientations include existential/humanistic, interpersonal relationship, psychoanalytical, rational/emotive, Gestalt, social learning, systems oriented, and transactional analysis.

Client-centered Counseling

Client-centered or person-centered counseling derives from the work of Carl Rogers. Its importance is understood most easily in light of the situation that prevailed in the 1940s when Rogers first began to publish. At that time, guidance was closely associated with testing. Rogers, whose theories derive in part from the experience of psychotherapists (he was one), stressed that the client, rather than the test, should be at the center of counseling. A client-centered approach sees the warm, trusting relationship between counselor and client as crucial to the success of the counseling. To establish such a relationship, the counselor must accept the client's perception of a situation rather than rely on outside measures, such as tests. In philosophy, the idea that a person's perceptions are the only reality is a basic thesis of phenomenology; thus, this approach is sometimes called phenomenological.

Behavioral Counseling

Behavioral counseling derives from the work of psychologists such as B.F. Skinner. The client decides on the change in behavior sought, but the counselor determines the techniques and procedures to be used. The counselor can even be seen as manipulating the client. Behavioral therapy has been very successful in dealing with some problems, such as stress, in which relief of symptoms is sufficient.

Psychoanalytical Approaches

Psychoanalytical approaches to counseling derive from Sigmund Freud's theories of human nature. According to Freud, people have psychological problems when their ego (or conscious self) fails to balance their id (desire for pleasure) against their superego (the thundering NO! of society).

Existentialism

Existentialism can refer to the somewhat different philosophies of various writers, including Jean Paul Sartre, Albert Camus, Martin Heidegger, and Soren Kierkegaard. In counseling, an existential approach aims at the clients' accepting responsibility for their own actions.

Rational-Emotive Approaches

Rational-emotive or cognitive approaches share with existentialism an emphasis on the individual's responsibility for self-development. Its particular emphasis is that the individual takes control through reason. Among its proponents is Albert Ellis.

Classifications such as those used here always carry the danger that they will be applied too rigidly. In the earlier chapters, you have seen counselors taking various approaches to different problems. In reading over these approaches, you have probably thought of cases in which different theories would be most effective. Indeed, according to Dr. Herr's testimony, researchers have found that, "Regardless of the different theoretical positions that guide the specific techniques used by particular counselors, counselors found to be therapeutic in their interactions with counselees tend to share many common characteristics." An eclectic approach is most often mentioned in every survey. Less important than the philosophical basis of the counselor are the basic principles of guidance—the recognition of the dignity and worth of the individual and the acceptance of the individual's right to choose her or his own future.

INTERVIEWING AND GROUP COUNSELING

Besides a concern with theory, counselor trainees should be aware of the techniques used by counselors. Interviews and group sessions are the tools most often used.

Examples of well-conducted interviews appear frequently in counseling journals and in the books on counseling listed in appendix B. The principles are easily summarized. Counselors must prepare in advance by reviewing the client's records or consulting with others. The counselor should put the client at ease. The reason for the client's presence should then be established, but the counselor must be aware that the stated reason is not always the real reason. The counselor must let the client take the lead in the interview; this is accomplished by asking open questions and by reflecting what the client says rather than the counselor introducing his or her own ideas. As the interview progresses, the counselor encourages the client to consider the next step to be taken—a test, an action, a review of the problem. The client then may summarize what has been accomplished in the interview. The counselor accompanies the client to the door.

Group counseling has many advantages in certain situations. It enables the counselor to work with more people in less time, establishes peer relationships among the counselees, and sometimes leads them to accept suggestions from each other that they would not entertain from the counselor. Groups work well for individuals who can talk about their concerns, need the reactions of others, and find the support of their peers helpful. They also benefit those who need to develop social skills or get in touch with other people. The determination of who can benefit from group sessions is one of the most difficult for a counselor to make.

CHAPTER 17

CURRENT ISSUES IN COUNSELING

The present is big with the future.

—Leibnitz

One of the things that is not new under the sun is that professions change as society develops new needs. Once we needed horse traders; now we rely on automobile sales representatives. Counseling, too, is subject to changes in society. Some of these changes, such as the growing size of the adult population, are certain. Others, such as the payment of counselors by insurers, are not. These changes have raised important issues for counseling. Other important issues concerning the education that counselors need and the proper role for counselors in society are as old as the occupation. They are not likely to be resolved anytime soon.

THIRD-PARTY PAYMENT

Factors such as the changing age structure of the population and new technology—which may result in more career switching—are fueling possible changes in the rate of growth for particular specialties and increasing the types of settings in which counselors are employed. Demand for services does not necessarily mean that the services will be purchased, however. Not all who want a new car can afford to buy one. The actual growth of counseling, therefore, depends not only on the number of potential clients but also on their willingness and ability to pay for counseling services. It is not possible to gauge the degree of either. However, there would be a greater stimulus to growth if people were able to pay for counseling indirectly—through health insurance, for example. It is for this reason that the question of third-party payment—the payment of the counselor by someone other than the client—is so important.

Third-party payment is already somewhat common. Almost 60 percent of the certified clinical mental health counselors responding to a recent survey received third-party payments. In some cases, payment is made through another professional. For example, a counselor may provide services in partnership with a physician. The insurer reimburses the physician who, in turn, pays the counselor.

Counselors are not now reimbursed under Medicare or Medicaid programs, although language authorizing such payments has been written into bills before Congress. The passage of such a bill into law would have a major impact on the growth of private practice in counseling both in itself and because it would legitimize third-party payments by other major insurers such as Blue Cross. The speed with which the situation is changing is indicated by the fact that since the first edition of this book in 1986, Congress has authorized the payment of counselors by CHAMPUS, the agency that pays civilian practitioners for medical services performed for members of the military services and their dependents. But payments are made only to counselors who are licensed or certified.

LICENSURE AND CERTIFICATION

Implementation of third-party payment plans adds pressure to bring about strict licensure laws. In general, a license specifies the activities that a person in a given occupation can perform. Certification, which is similar, defines the standards that a person must meet in order to use a job title. Frequently, a license to practice is granted by a government agency while certification is controlled by an association of practitioners.

The term *counselor* is now defined in twenty-nine states, although in the others you can still see signs that read "Madame Zodiac—Palm Reading and Marriage Counseling." The first state licensure law was passed in Virginia in 1976. Since then, such laws have been passed in the following states: Alabama, Arizona, Arkansas, Colorado, Delaware, Florida, Georgia, Idaho, Kansas, Louisiana, Maryland, Massachusetts, Michigan, Mississippi, Missouri, Montana, Nebraska, North Carolina, Ohio, Oklahoma, Rhode Island, South Carolina, Tennessee, Texas, Vermont, Washington, West Virginia, and Wyoming. The addresses of the licensing boards for these states are listed in appendix C.

Although laws do vary, among the common key provisions, from the point of view of a person planning to become a counselor, is graduation from a master's program accredited by the Council for Accreditation of Counseling and Related Educational Programs. These programs require forty-eight semester hours (as opposed to the thirty-three to forty hours required in most programs), a practicum lasting sixty contact hours, and an internship lasting three hundred contact hours; another option for certification is to have two years of experience and course work in six of the eight following areas: human growth and development; social and cultural foundations; the helping relationship; group dynamics, processing, and counseling; life-style and career development; appraisal of individuals; research and evaluation; and professional orientation. Under either option, candidates for certification must pass an exam, have three thousand hours of supervised counseling experience, and provide professional assessments from two colleagues or supervisors. Many other bodies offer certification of different kinds, and many counselors hold more than one certificate. The different boards are listed with the various counseling occupations and in appendix C.

Licensure has many ramifications, not all of which are predictable at this time. For example, the standards may come to be applied to programs for school counselors as well as for those who wish to work in private practice or community agencies. Questions concerning reciprocity of state-recognized certificates and teaching requirements for counselors in educational settings are also frequently debated. Opposition to the laws is not unknown. It comes from local psychological associations in some cases; in at least one case, a rehabilitation services company opposed the legislation. A shortage of counselors would also undermine licensure. In a discussion of the employment trends for school psychologists, Thomas Fagan writes,

> Too large a discrepancy in supply and demand (e.g., 10–20 percent) would pose an unfortunate dilemma among the agencies and persons controlling training, credentialing, and practice. Unmet demand would trigger altered credential requirements for school-based employees. To maintain practical existence in the long-run, professional organizations could be forced to relax the progress for increased standards made in recent decades.

To summarize, the current trend is toward increasing licensure requirements, but the future is, as ever, uncertain.

COUNSELING, PSYCHIATRY, AND PSYCHOLOGY

Within guidance and counseling, there is a continuity between simply providing information and enabling a client to use the information, which might require techniques resembling psychotherapy. The principles of guidance and psychology are indeed closely related and, according to Nancy Scott, the Association for Counselor Education and Supervision president in 1987, confusion of the two continues. Where a particular counselor fits along the line depends on the nature of the problems that clients bring to him or her. Clients seeking to change careers, for example, rarely need to change the way they live. Clients who regularly overeat or abuse alcohol, however, must be helped to change their behavior, just as a psychiatrist's patients often must behave differently to be considered cured. What then is the difference between counseling and psychiatry or psychology?

The border between counseling and therapy is less like a wall than a seashore. Counseling does indeed make use of techniques developed by therapists; it just does not follow them as far. Counselors, for example, would usually see a client fewer times than a therapist would see a patient.

One difference is hidden in the previous sentence. Counselors have clients; psychiatrists and psychologists have patients. The people seen by a counselor are not regarded as mentally ill either by themselves or the counselor. Another distinction is that counselors deal with normal transitions and adjustments. A counselor who suspects someone is ill or severely affected by his or her condition will refer that person to an appropriate psychiatrist or psychologist.

More clear than the difference in practice is the difference in preparation. A psychiatrist must be a doctor of medicine. A psychologist or counseling psychologist must usually have a Ph.D. A counselor usually has a master's degree.

The waters are stirred up a little more by the term *psychoanalysis*. Strictly speaking, it refers to the method of treatment for the mentally ill developed by Sigmund Freud. Patients undergoing psychoanalysis make an intensive study of their own past, especially of events in their childhood that they no longer remember consciously. Counselors do not practice psychoanalysis. Loosely speaking, some counseling work may be referred to as *psychotherapy,* a term that includes psychoanalysis and other methods of treatment. But this term too is best restricted to situations where someone is being treated for mental or emotional disorder.

THE COUNSELOR'S ROLE

Like the relationship between counseling and psychology, the relationship between counseling and guidance in the school is subject to constant dispute; the American School Counselor Association's role statements are being rewritten even as this book is being published. Indeed, each specialty seems to have its own controversy over the counselor's role. Rehabilitation counselors are torn between counseling and coordinating services of other providers such as medical practitioners and welfare agencies. Employment counselors must constantly struggle to avoid becoming no more than test administrators. In the elementary schools, to give a final example, some see the counselor's chief duty as consulting with teachers rather than counseling children.

None of these controversies is likely to be resolved anytime soon. Indeed, those that pit counselors against administrators will probably never be resolved. The most that someone entering the profession can hope to do is be aware of them.

CHAPTER 18

COUNSELING'S FUTURE

Good counselors lack no clients.

—Shakespeare

The social and technological developments that have changed so many occupations in recent years—increasing the demand for some, almost eliminating others, and changing the nature of the work in almost all—will also affect the future of counseling, although to what degree is largely a matter of speculation. At least two changes are certain: counselors will make greater use of computer technology and counselors will do more work with adults.

COMPUTERIZED COUNSELING

The impact of computers on counseling will probably be extensive. Their use in career education is already widespread, with many high school students being able to use computers to retrieve individualized information about colleges, training programs, and occupations with programs such as Career Focus. Already, more than half of all college planning/placement offices use computers for career guidance and counseling. Computers can also shorten the time needed to assess aptitudes because tests taken at computer terminals can be scored almost instantaneously. The General Aptitude Test used by the Employment Service, the Armed Services Vocational Aptitude tests, and many others can now be taken at a computer terminal. Interactive programs such as MORTON and PLATO DCS are even available for psychodiagnosis. Their practicality may be limited because only clients comfortable with computer keyboards can use them at present, but people comfortable with computers, such as students, prefer them to pencil and paper.

Naturally, counselors can also use computers to ease their recordkeeping, data analysis, and word-processing burdens. One survey found that 75 percent of counselor educators now use computers for word processing.

Computers cannot replace the counselor, of course, any more than the once ballyhooed teaching machine was able to replace live instructors. In the words of the College Entrance Examination Board's Commission on Precollege Guidance and Counseling, "Computers . . . should be viewed as extensions of rather than substitutes for counselors, giving counselors more time for the activities that are central to their role." Counselors can use the machines to make more information available both to their clients and to themselves, but the essential work of the counselor—clarifying, instructing, and motivating—still remains. Paradoxically, computers might even increase the need for personal counseling because a computer printout of test results has greater credibility, and clients must be cautioned concerning their use. J.P. Sampson, for example, warns that computers make giving tests too easy, tempting untrained administrators to give and misinterpret them.

MORE WORK WITH ADULTS

The social changes taking place are likely to have a much deeper impact than the use of computers. Several trends are important. The number of older people is growing rapidly, and the average life span is lengthening. Conrad Glass and Katherine Brant note that these trends "are creating conditions that require the expansion of counseling services to a segment of the population often overlooked—the adult who is 65 years old and older." The middle-aged population is also growing as the baby-boom generation works its way through the life cycle. One result of that trend will be a much larger number of people switching careers in mid-life, either through choice or necessity; counseling can assist many of these people in clarifying their goals and learning what their options are. Changes in marital relationships and other concerns might also stimulate demand for counseling in this segment of the population. The result of these various trends is that the number and proportion of counselors working with adults will almost certainly increase. One sign of these changes has already been seen at the American Association for Counseling and Development. Its Association for Adult Development and Aging did not exist four years ago; it now has two thousand members.

Counselors working for agencies or in private practices that are obviously aimed at adults will not be the only ones affected by this trend. For example, many college and community college counselors will increasingly meet adults. These counselors will have to adapt themselves to the different needs of adult students, who are likely to be more anxious to complete their education speedily—especially if it is required for a new career—while also having greater family responsibilities and economic pressures than the traditional college-age population.

COUNSELORS IN NEW SETTINGS: PRIVATE SECTOR, PRIVATE PRACTICE

Many changes are foreseen in counseling: more gerontological counseling, more career counseling for adults, more mental health counseling. Indeed, Hollis and Wantz argue that the unmodified term *counselor* is becoming dated; now the reference is to specific kinds of counselors, such as those described in this book. As these changes occur, employment will shift away from the schools. Counselors already work in a great variety of settings: mental health agencies, rehabilitation agencies, correctional facilities, public employment agencies, health care facilities, employment assistance and human resource development programs in business and industry, and private practice. The variety of settings may not increase, but, in the opinion of many people in the field, the number of counselors employed outside the schools will, perhaps dramatically. In particular, most authorities expect to see more counselors employed by businesses and community agencies and many more entering private practice.

Although the extent of this growth is problematic, some developments along these lines have already taken place. For example, the enrollment of people in counselor education programs designed to prepare people for positions other than school counselor is now four times the enrollment in school counselor programs—which have, in fact, been declining for the past ten years. Surveys of graduates of counselor education programs also indicate that a substantial percentage are not working in schools. In one survey of more than a thousand graduates, over twice as many were employed outside the schools as in them. Graduates of a gerontological program were employed in state agencies, area agencies on aging, senior residence centers, mental health centers, and long-term care facilities.

Evidence also points toward more employment in business and more self-employment. Between 1950 and 1987, the number of employee assistance programs grew from about fifty to ten thousand. Only 3 percent or so of mental health counselors work for employee assistance programs or in business settings, but these programs often refer employees to treatment programs where counselors work. Department stores even employ counselors to work with customers who have problems handling credit. Articles on career counseling for adults also indicate the change, for besides school-based programs, they are likely to list services sponsored by community agencies and private practices as sources of help. A periodical, *Private Practice News,* is devoted to these counselors. Perhaps the clearest sign of change is that the mental health division of the AACD—which did not even exist a few years ago—now has twelve thousand members. Many of these counselors—perhaps 25 percent or more—are in private practice, as shown by a survey conducted by William Weikel, Richard Daniel, and Janet Anderson and by the AACD's annual survey of members.

CHAPTER 19

ADVICE FROM THE EXPERTS

In conducting the research for this book, I had the chance to speak to a large number of counselors in a variety of settings. At the end of each conversation, I asked them for advice, suggestions, or other comments they would like to make to someone who was considering a career in counseling. The following are their replies, listed alphabetically. In 1989, when I asked them if their remarks were still valid, most said that their statements should be even more forceful now.

> A growing field in vocational assessment and counseling is the rehabilitation area. Take a good look at it.
> —Olie Ahlquist, Past President, National Employment Counselors Association

> I've often found that people looking for a job do not know what that job entails. I'd recommend that you talk to a rehabilitation counselor—or a counselor in any other field that you are considering entering—and watch one at work, if possible.
> —Les Blankenship, Vocational Rehabilitation Program Specialist, Rehabilitation Services Administration, U.S. Department of Education

> Counseling and student affairs offer many career possibilities other than in the elementary and secondary school—learn about

them and try to explore them all. College students should seek out work experiences in student affairs.

—William A. Bryan, Past President, American College Personnel Association

Student affairs workers who like their jobs say they enjoy the environment of an institution of higher education, enjoy working with people, and enjoy the variety of contacts with students and faculty members.

—Jon Dalton, Assistant Vice-President for Student Affairs, Northern Illinois University

With regard to sex education and counseling, first seek an education in counseling, psychology, or social work; and then, after accumulating years of experience, you can try to specialize in human sexuality.

—Tom Gertz, Past President, American Association of Sex Educators, Counselors, and Therapists

If you are considering counseling as a career, ask yourself first how important freedom of choice for the individual is to you; if it's not of major importance, reconsider your career choice.

—Ken Hoyt, Kansas State University

Counseling will be on the cutting edge of assisting students to cope with the stress of the modern age so that they can fulfill their academic potential. With excellent training in all the new counseling skills, you will have many options—but you'll have to be skilled at working with families and the special concerns of today's young people: substance abuse, unemployment, teenage pregnancy, suicide, and all the others.

—Dorothy Jenkins, State Director, Guidance and Counseling, D.C. Public Schools; Past President, American School Counselor Association

Student affairs in community colleges is very competitive and has no clear career ladder, but it is full of challenges and rewards.

—John Keyser, President, Clakamas Community College

The end result of rehabilitation in the private sector is to return the client to gainful employment. This requires that the counselor must develop close relations with employers; and to do that means you must understand business so that you can match their clients with individual employers. A counselor must also understand the legal system, because rehabilitation services are often delivered as a legal benefit within the insurance system.

—Richard LaFon, Executive Director, National Association of Rehabilitation Professionals in the Private Sector

In a field like financial aid—or student personnel generally—you must be ready for change, which is both the drawback and the satisfaction of the job.

—Dennis Martin, Director of Financial Aid, Washington University

After looking at this book, quickly go out and find some working counselors who can give you first-hand experience about what the job is like. Get some part-time experience—even as a volunteer—in a variety of counseling settings.

—Carl McDaniels, Virginia Polytechnic Institute and State University

Growth in social support occupations—such as rehabilitation and other counseling fields—will be very strong if our society continues to develop along the lines of one person's having several careers in a lifetime. The need for experts who can identify how a person's skills and aptitudes will fit new occupations could be substantial.

—Frederick E. Menz, The University of Wisconsin-Stout

Explore; start early—meet people through professional organizations, talk to them, and gain work experience.

—Fred Otte, Georgia State University

If you are thinking about becoming a pastoral counselor, first ask if you wish to serve people in the ministry, then ask if you wish to serve the ministry as a counselor.

—Duane Parker, Executive Director, Association for Clinical Pastoral Education

A career decision begins with self-assessment. Learn about the occupation but learn also about your own needs and values. Volunteer experiences and talking to professional counselors about their work should help you learn if you'll find potential satisfaction in the work.

—Bill K. Richardson, North Texas State University

Every year, the responsibilities of school counselors grow, in keeping with their general mandate of promoting academic success for all students; we now deal with suicide prevention, child abuse, study skills, substance abuse, test-taking techniques, stress, anxiety, and drop-out and truancy prevention. This combination should make the demand for well-trained school counselors rise in the coming years. At the same time, the number of people being trained for educational settings is declining.

—Dr. Dorothy Thomas, Past President, American School Counselor Association

School counselors in the future will probably have larger caseloads, making it more important than ever that you develop your skills as a consultant so that you can work with parents, teachers, and other school professionals in order to serve the students.

—Jean A. Thompson, Past President, American Association for Counseling and Development and American School Counselor Association

If you like to work with people, the satisfaction of counseling is great. The lengthening education and continuing education requirements should be considered, however; they will make it more difficult to become a counselor but might also increase the salaries and prestige of the profession in the long run.

—Edwin A. Whitfield, Director of School Guidance, State of Ohio

You should seek to be highly competent and especially well trained in a variety of counseling techniques because of the changes now taking place in the delivery of, and payment for, mental health services.

—Richard R. Wilmarth, Chairperson, National Academy of Certified Clinical Mental Health Counselors

The need for assessing an individual's skills and matching employers with employees will continue to be met in some way by our society, although the agencies that now utilize employment counselors may change.

—Gaynelle Wilson, Past President, National Employment Counselors Association

A background in rehabilitation counseling can provide a springboard to the broader industry involved in containing the costs of health care—but you'll have to prod your graduate school into preparing you for the private sector.

—Jim Wilson, Past President, National Association of Rehabilitation Professionals in the Private Sector

If you are considering becoming a rehabilitation counselor, try to enter an undergraduate rehabilitation feeder program—it can save a semester or more at the graduate level.

—George Wright, The University of Wisconsin, Madison

Top: A mental health counselor discusses career options in her field with students. (Chicago Department of Mental Health photo) *Bottom:* Group counseling enables counselors to work with more people in less time. (Sinclair Community College photo, Mike Inderrieden, photographer)

CHAPTER 20

CODA: COUNSELING, A HEALING PROFESSION

> Give a hungry man a fish and he can eat for a day; teach a hungry man to fish and he can eat all his life.
>
> —Proverb

The glamour of heart surgery does not shine around counseling. "Counselors care," this book proclaims at its opening. And a cold world responds, "Who cares?" Ours is not an age of sensibility. We are a practical people concerned less with caring than with curing, less with helping than with healing. The challenge of counseling now and tomorrow will be to develop its potential to heal.

Richard Bolles, the author of *What Color Is Your Parachute?*, issued this challenge to the profession in a speech at the American Personnel and Guidance Association convention in 1983. He suggested that counseling could be content with service or could move on to empower people. "It is one thing," he said, "to throw a drowning person a rope. It is another to see a person in crisis and seize that as the moment to show them how to take control of the crisis, to teach them how to get out of the crisis for the rest of their lives."

He went on to refer to his well-known book, asking rhetorically why it is so successful. The book, after all, deals with what would seem to be the most pedestrian of counseling activities—finding a job—and it has no lack of competitors. Bolles pointed out that in reality *Parachute* is a book of healing; it only masquerades as a job-hunting manual. It heals the reader's self-esteem; it repairs the blow to their sense of worth when an employer says, "I don't need you; I don't want you!"

Like the rest of us, counselors are inundated by information and technological change. But more machines and more knowledge will not make counseling much more effective. "The future of counseling," Bolles concluded, "does not depend on mastering information or technology but in mastering ourselves as healers."

APPENDIX A

NATIONAL ASSOCIATIONS AND CERTIFICATION AUTHORITIES

Associations can provide three types of useful information for people interested in careers. First, they almost always publish a directory that will give you the names of nearby practitioners that you can talk with about the job. Second, their newsletters, journals, and other publications often contain want ads, articles about salaries and employment or other developments, and case studies based on actual situations that can give you insight into the nature of the work. Third, they sometimes publish pamphlets about occupations. The certification authorities publish registers of certified practitioners and booklets explaining the certification requirements. The accrediting authorities for educational programs are listed in the chapter on education.

A few of the associations listed here have such similar names that they may seem to be the same organization. Some of the apparent duplication is due to the character of a parent body; for example, the American Rehabilitation Counseling Association is specifically concerned with rehabilitation within the American Association for Counseling and Development, while the National Rehabilitation Counseling Association represents counselors within the National Rehabilitation Association.

American Association for Counseling and Development
 5999 Stevenson Avenue
 Alexandria, Virginia 22304
 (703) 823-9800

With more than fifty-four thousand members, this is the largest association of counselors in the country. It publishes the *Journal of Counseling and Development, Guidepost,* and many monographs and pamphlets. The Association has fifteen divisions and organizational affiliates that, in the words of its membership pamphlet, "span counseling and human development work at all educational levels from kindergarten through higher education, in community agencies, correctional agencies, rehabilitation programs, government, business/industry, and research facilities." The association does not provide financial aid or counseling services to individuals. The following are among its divisions and their publications (the number of members appears in parentheses):

- American College Personnel Association (7,500–8,000)—*Journal of College Student Development; ACPA Developments*
- Association for Counselor Education and Supervision (2,500–3,000)—*Counselor Education and Supervision; ACES Spectrum*
- National Career Development Association (5,500–6,500)—*The Career Development Quarterly; NCDA Newsletter*
- Association for Humanistic Education and Development (3,000–4,000)—*The Journal of Humanistic Education and Development; Infochange*
- American School Counselor Association (9,000–10,000)—*The School Counselor; Elementary School Guidance and Counseling; The ASCA Counselor*
- American Rehabilitation Counseling Association (2,500–3,500)—*Rehabilitation Counseling Bulletin; The ARCA News*
- Association for Measurement and Evaluation in Counseling and Development (1,500–2,500)—*Measurement and Evaluation in Counseling and Development; AMECD Newsnotes*
- National Employment Counselors Association (1,500–2,000)—*Journal of Employment Counseling; NECA Newsletter*
- Association for Multicultural Counseling and Development (2,000–2,500)—*Journal of Multicultural Counseling and Development; AMCD Newsletter*
- Association for Religious and Value Issues in Counseling (3,500–4,500)—*Counseling and Values; ARVIC Interaction*

- Association for Specialists in Group Work (4,500–5,500)—*Journal for Specialists in Group Work; Together*
- American Mental Health Counselors Association (11,500–12,500)—*Journal of Mental Health Counseling, AMHCA News*
- Public Offender Counselor Association (an organizational affiliate, 1,500–2,000)—*Journal of Offender Counseling; POCA Report*
- Military Educators and Counselors Association (750–1,000)—*MECA Newsletter*
- Association for Adult Development and Aging (1,500–2,000)—*AADA Newsletter*

American Association for Marriage and Family Therapy
1717 K Street, NW
Washington, D.C. 20006
(202) 429-1825

The 14,500 members are drawn from several disciplines, including medicine and counseling. It publishes a bimonthly newspaper, a quarterly journal, and a biennial membership register.

American Association of Pastoral Counselors
9508A Lee Highway
Fairfax, Virginia 22031
(703) 385-6967

An association of three thousand ministers, priests, rabbis, and other religiously oriented counselors and professionals. It publishes a newsletter that lists job and training opportunities and is copublisher of *The Journal of Pastoral Care*. The Council on Ministry in Specialized Settings, at the same address, has a guide to other associations of pastoral care and counseling, such as the National Association of Catholic Chaplains and the Chaplaincy Commission, New York Board of Rabbis.

American Association of Sex Educators, Counselors and Therapists
11 Dupont Circle, NW, Suite 220
Washington, D.C. 20036
(202) 462-1171

A multidisciplinary association of about three thousand physicians, psychologists, ministers, counselors, social workers, educators, marriage and family therapists, and others engaged in sex education, counseling, and therapy. It publishes a quarterly *Journal of Sex Education and Therapy*, a monthly newsletter, and an annual register of certified sex educators, sex counselors, and sex therapists. Its address may soon change.

American Psychological Association
1200 17th Street, NW
Washington, D.C. 20036
(202) 833-7000

A society of scientists, teachers, and professionals organized to advance psychology (fifty-two thousand members). Membership is largely restricted to those who hold the doctorate. The concerns of counselors and members of the APA overlap at numerous points. The association has forty divisions, four of which are directly related to counseling: Division 15, Educational Psychology; Division 16, School Psychology; Division 17, Counseling Psychology; Division 22, Rehabilitation Psychology. It publishes "Careers in Psychology," "Delivery of Services by Counseling Psychologists," and "Delivery of Services by School Psychologists" (single copies free) among many other items, including the following periodicals: *American Psychologist, Journal of Counseling Psychology, Journal of Educational Psychology, APA Monitor, The Educational Psychologist* (Division 15), *School Psychology Monograph* (Division 16), *The Counseling Psychologist* (Division 17), *Rehabilitation Psychology* (Division 22).

American Society for Training and Development
  1630 Duke Street
  Box 1443
  Alexandria, Virginia 22313
  (703) 683-8100

An association of twenty-three thousand practitioners, managers, administrators, educators, and researchers in human resources development. Members design and implement employee and organization development programs in a broad range of business, education, government, and service organizations. It publishes a monthly magazine, *Training and Development Journal,* a monthly newspaper, *National Report,* directories of members and consultants, and numerous books, including the *ASTD Directory of Academic Programs,* second edition, Ruth Gentilman, editor. Members can join a professional practice area, one of which—career development—is for members who provide people and their organizations with guidance in the application of career development systems; they balance the needs of the employer and the employee so that the goals of both are met.

American Vocational Association
  1410 King Street
  Alexandria, Virginia 22314
  (703) 522-6121

This is a very large, forty-three-thousand-member association of teachers and others interested in vocational education. Among its many divisions are ones devoted to employment and training and guidance. It publishes the *Vocational Education Journal.*

College Placement Council, Inc.
  62 Highland Avenue
  Bethlehem, Pennsylvania 18017
  (215) 868-1421

An association for career counseling and placement directors and representatives of employers of college graduates in business, industry, and government. The placement offices on college campuses often have copies of its publications if the library does not. It publishes *The Journal of College Placement* (quarterly), *Spotlight* (a biweekly newsletter), a membership directory, and "Looking for a Career?" (a six-panel pamphlet on the field of career planning and placement) as well as many other items.

Board for Rehabilitation Certification
 1156 Shure Drive, Suite 350
 Arlington Heights, Illinois 60004
 (312) 394-2104

This board certifies and provides information concerning the certification of rehabilitation counselors and insurance rehabilitation specialists.

Independent Educational Consultants Association
 Cove Road, P.O. Box 125
 Forestdale, Massachusetts 02644
 (508) 477-2127

An association of educational counselors in private practice. It publishes a membership directory.

National Academy of Certified Clinical Mental Health Counselors
 5999 Stevenson Avenue
 Alexandria, Virginia 22304
 (703) 823-9800

This board certifies clinical mental health counselors. It publishes a newsletter. Certification may be required for third-party payment.

National Association of Alcoholism and Drug Abuse Counselors
  951 South George Mason Drive, Suite 204
  Arlington, Virginia 22204
  (703) 920-4644

The eleven thousand members of this association work in hospitals, treatment centers, private practice, councils and agencies on alcoholism and drug abuse, and employee assistance programs. It publishes *The Counselor,* a bimonthly magazine.

National Association of Rehabilitation Professionals in the Private Sector
  P.O. Box 708
  Twin Peaks, California 92391
  (714) 337-0746

An association of rehabilitation counselors and the firms they work for in the private sector. It publishes a code of ethics and a bimonthly newsletter, *NARPPS News*.

National Association of School Psychologists, Inc.
  Suite 200
  808 17th Street, NW
  Washington, D.C. 20006
  (202) 223-9498

An association for school psychologists (fifteen thousand members). It publishes *School Psychology Review* (quarterly) and a newsletter.

National Association of Student Activity Advisers
  1904 Association Drive
  Reston, Virginia 22091
  (703) 860-0200

A seven-thousand-member association of directors of student activities, deans, and others affiliated with student activity programs in middle schools and high schools. It publishes *Leadership for Student Activities* (monthly) and other material.

National Association of Student Financial Aid Administrators
   1920 L Street, NW, Suite 200
   Washington, D.C. 20036
   (202) 785-0453

An association of institutions and financial aid administrators with thirty-five hundred members. It publishes a monthly newsletter and the *Journal of Student Financial Aid*.

National Association of Student Personnel Administrators, Inc.
   1700 18th Street, NW
   Washington, D.C. 20009
   (202) 265-7500

An association of five thousand student affairs officers in postsecondary institutions and interested graduate students. Publications include the *NASPA Journal*, *NASPA Forum* (its newsletter), and an annual salary survey.

National Association of Substance Abuse Trainers and Educators
   c/o Southern University at New Orleans
   6400 Press Drive
   New Orleans, Louisiana 70126
   (504) 282-4401

A relatively small association of academic, state, and federal trainers who voluntarily exchange information on substance abuse/chemical dependency training in higher education with respect to courses, student populations, degree programs, nondegree programs, and graduate studies. The major activity of the association is to sustain a clearinghouse of training and educational opportunities.

National Board for Certified Counselors, Inc.
5999 Stevenson Avenue
Alexandria, Virginia 22304
(703) 461-6222

This board certifies counselors who have voluntarily sought certification and maintains a register. It offers both a generic certification and a specialized certification for career counselors. This certification does not constitute a license to practice in states that have passed counselor licensure legislation.

National Rehabilitation Counseling Association
633 South Washington Street
Alexandria, Virginia 22314
(703) 836-7677

Part of the National Rehabilitation Association, it has forty-three hundred members. It publishes the *Journal of Applied Rehabilitation Counseling*.

APPENDIX B

BOOKS ABOUT COLLEGE, GRADUATE SCHOOL, CAREERS, AND COUNSELING

The following two selective lists contain two kinds of books. The first has general works for job hunters and career seekers, including a couple of books on selecting a college and scholarships. The second has books about counseling. Several are used as a text in an introductory course; they provide insight into the methods used in counseling and the concerns counselors deal with.

GENERAL BOOKS ON COLLEGE AND CAREERS

American Universities and Colleges. Washington, D.C.: American Council on Education. annual.

Bloch, Deborah Perlmutter. *How to Get and Get Ahead on Your First Job.* Lincolnwood, Ill.: VGM Career Horizons, 1988. Step-by-step details on how to get a first job.

―――. *How to Have a Winning Job Interview.* Lincolnwood, Ill.: VGM Career Horizons, 1987. Advice on how to win an interview and get a job.

―――. *How to Write a Winning Résumé.* Lincolnwood, Ill.: VGM Career Horizons, 1989. Filled with tips and examples.

Bolles, Richard N. *What Color Is Your Parachute? A Practical Manual for Job-Hunters and Career-Changers.* Berkeley, Calif.: Ten Speed Press, 1983 (but new editions frequent). Quite possibly the most frequently recommended guide to finding a career (not just a job).

Chronicle Guide to Graduate and Professional Study. Moravia, N.Y.: Chronicle Guidance Publications, Inc. biennial.

The College Handbook Index of Majors. Princeton, N.J.: College Board Publications. annual.

A Guide to Graduate Study. Washington, D.C.: American Council on Education. frequent editions.

Kennedy, Joyce Lain and Darryl Laramore. *Joyce Lain Kennedy's Career Book*. Lincolnwood, Ill.: VGM Career Horizons, 1988. Covers deciding what you want to do, moving on from your present job, and everything in between.

Lott, Catherine S. and Oscar C. Lott. *How to Land a Better Job*. Lincolnwood, Ill.: VGM Career Horizons, 1989. Covers everything from finding leads to negotiating salaries.

Lovejoy's College Guide. Red Bank, N.J.: Lovejoy's College Guide, Inc. frequent editions.

Michelozzi, Betty Neville. *Coming Alive from Nine to Five*. Palo Alto, Calif.: Mayfield Publishing Co., 1984. Career planning, with exercises for self-assessment.

Need a Lift? Indianapolis: The American Legion. An annual hundred-page plus listing of current information on careers, loans, and scholarships.

Peterson's Guides: Graduate Study. 4 vols. Princeton, N.J.: Peterson's Guides. annual.

Rubinfeld, William A. *Planning Your College Education*. Lincolnwood, Ill.: VGM Career Horizons, 1982. Discusses choosing and gaining admission to college.

U.S. Department of Labor. *Occupational Outlook Handbook*. Washington, D.C.: Government Printing Office. biennial. Considerable information on 225 occupations, counseling and psychology among them. It has updated information on employment, salaries, and outlook.

BOOKS ABOUT COUNSELING

Brown, Jeannette A. and Robert H. Pate, Jr., eds. *Being a Counselor*. Monterey, Calif.: Brooks Cole, 1983.

Burks, Mary Paxton. *Requirements for Certification: Teachers, Counselors, Librarians, Administrators, for Elementary Schools, Secondary Schools, Junior Colleges*. 51st ed. Chicago: University of Chicago Press, 1988.

Gysbers, Norman and associates. *Designing Careers*. San Francisco: Jossey-Bass, 1984. This is a third decennial review of career counseling put together by the National Association for Career Counseling and Development, formerly the National Vocational Guidance Association. The contributors, a virtual who's who of the field, include Norman Gysbers, C. Gilbert Wrenn, Donald E. Super, Harold Goldstein, Edwin L. Herr, Johnie H. Miles, Howard E. Figler, Carl McDaniels, and many others.

Gysbers, Norman C. and P. Henderson. *Organizing and Managing School Guidance Programs: Leadership Skills for the 1990's*. Alexandria, Va.: American Association for Counseling and Development, 1988.

Herr, Edwin L. and Nancy M. Pinson, eds. *Foundation for Policy in Guidance and Counseling*. Alexandria, Va.: American Association for Counseling and Development, 1982.

Hummel, Dean L. and Charles W. Humes. *Pupil Services: Development, Coordination, Administration*. New York: Macmillan, 1984.

Mortensen, Donald and Alan Schmuller. *Guidance in Today's School*. New York: John Wiley and Sons, 1976.

Pietrofesa, John J., et al. *Counseling: An Introduction*. 2d ed. Boston: Houghton Mifflin, 1984.

Shertzer, Bruce and Shelley C. Stone. *Fundamentals of Counseling*. 3d ed. Boston: Houghton Mifflin, 1981.

Super, Donald E. and Charles M. Super. *Opportunities in Psychology Careers*. Lincolnwood, Ill.: VGM Career Horizons, 1988. A complete guide to the work of psychologists, including school psychologists, and ways to start out in the field.

Thompson, Charles L. and Linda B. Rudolph. *On Counseling Children*. 2d ed. Pacific Grove, Calif.: Brooks Cole, 1988.

Tolbert, E.L. *An Introduction to Guidance: The Professional Counselor*. 2d ed. Boston: Little Brown, 1982.

Whiteley, John M., et al. *The Coming Decade in Counseling Psychology*. Schenectady, N.Y.: Character Research Press, 1984.

Wright, George Nelson. *Total Rehabilitation*. Boston: Little Brown and Co., 1980. A very complete review of every aspect of rehabilitation as a service and as an occupation.

APPENDIX C

STATE ACCREDITING AND LICENSING AUTHORITIES

For each state the accreditation authority for school counselors is listed as well as other accrediting boards, such as for marriage and family counseling. The list is derived from information from the departments of education and from material provided by the American Association for Counseling and Development, the American Association for Marriage and Family Therapy, and the Certification Reciprocity Consortium/ Alcoholism and Other Drug Abuse, Inc.

Alabama

Teacher Certification Section
 State Department of Education
 349 State Office Building
 Montgomery 36130
 (205) 261-5060
 (School Counselors)

Dr. Donald Schmitz, Administrator
 Alabama Board of Examiners in Counseling
 P.O. Box 457
 Jacksonville 36265
 (205) 231-5472
 (Counselors in Nonschool Settings)

Alaska

Coordinator of Teacher Education and Certification
 State Department of Education
 P.O. Box F
 Juneau 99811
 (907) 465-2831
 (School Counselors)

Alaska Alcohol and Drug Abuse Counselor Certification Review Board
 3605 Arctic Boulevard #695
 Anchorage 99503
 (907) 243-1181
 (Alcohol and Drug Abuse Counselors)

Arizona

Arizona Department of Education
1535 West Jefferson
Room 126
Phoenix 85007
(602) 542-4367 (recorded message)
(602) 542-4368 (to request application)
(School Counselors)

Boards for counselors in nonschool settings and for marriage and family therapists are to be established.

Arkansas

Teacher Education and Certification
State Department of Education
Little Rock 72201
(501) 682-4342
(School Counselors)

Ms. Ann K. Thomas
Executive Secretary
Counselor Education Department
Southern Arkansas University
P.O. Box 1396
Magnolia 71753
(501) 234-4057
(Counselors in Nonschool Settings)

Arkansas Substance Abuse Certification Board
P.O. Box 962
North Little Rock 72115
(501) 758-8636
(Alcohol and Drug Abuse Counselors)

California

Commission for Teacher Preparation and Licensing
1812 9th Street
Sacramento 94244-2700
(916) 445-0185
(School Counselors)

Board of Behavioral Science Examiners
Room A-198
1021 O Street
Sacramento 95814
Attn: Kathleen Callanan
(916) 445-4933
(Marriage and Family Therapists)

California Association of Alcohol and Drug Abuse Counselors
1713 J Street
Suite 207
Sacramento 95814
(916) 447-9412
(Alcohol and Drug Abuse Counselors)

Colorado

Teacher Education and Certification
State Department of Education
201 East Colfax Avenue
Denver 80203
(303) 866-6851
(School Counselors)

Ginny Berry
2501 South Dahlia Street
Denver 80222
(303) 756-5644
(Counselors in Nonschool Settings)

State Board of Marriage and Family Therapist Examiners
Department of Regulatory Agencies
1525 Sherman Street, #128
Denver 80203
Attn: P.J. Hoffman, Sr., Administrative Clerk
(303) 866-3248
(Marriage and Family Therapists)

Connecticut

Bureau of Teacher Preparation and Certification
State Department of Education
165 Capitol Avenue
P.O. Box 2219
Hartford 06145
(203) 566-5201
(School Counselors)

Marriage and Family Therapy Certification
Department of Health Services
150 Washington Street
Hartford 06106
Attn: Alex Rodriguez
(203) 566-1039
(Marriage and Family Therapists)

Connecticut Alcohol and Drug Abuse Counselor Certification Board
416 New London Turnpike
Glastonbury 06033
(203) 633-6572
(Alcohol and Drug Abuse Counselors)

Delaware

Certification Office
Department of Public Instruction
P.O. Box 1402
Dover 19903
(302) 736-4686
(School Counselors)

Delaware Alcohol and Drug Abuse Counselor Certification Board, Inc.
P.O. Box 9937
Newark 19714-9937
(no phone)
(Alcohol and Drug Abuse Counselors)

A board for counselors in nonschool settings is to be established.

District of Columbia

Chief Examiner, Board of Examiners
District of Columbia Public Schools
Room 1004
415 12th Street, NW
Washington, DC 20004
(202) 924-4230
(School Counselors)

Washington Metropolitan Area Counselor Certification Board
2001 O Street, NW
Washington, DC 20036
(202) 393-0371
(Alcohol and Drug Abuse Counselors)

Florida

Bureau of Teacher Education and Certification
State Department of Education
B34 Collins Building
Tallahassee 32304
(904) 488-5701
(School Counselors)

Ms. Linda Biederman
Psychological Services/MFT
Department of Professional Regulations
Mental Health Counselor
130 Monroe Street
Tallahassee 32301
(904) 487-2520
(Counselors in Nonschool Settings and Marriage and Family Therapists)

Certification Board for Addiction Professionals of Florida
835B East Park Avenue
Tallahassee 32301
(904) 222-6314
(Alcohol and Drug Abuse Counselors)

Georgia

Georgia Department of Education
Division of Teacher Education and Certification
1452 Twin Towers East
Atlanta 30334
(404) 656-2406
(School Counselors)

Lori Gold, Director
Composite Board of Professional Counselors, Social Workers, and Marriage & Family Therapists
Examining Boards Division
166 Pryor Street, SW
Atlanta 30303
(404) 656-3989
(Counselors in Nonschool Settings and Marriage and Family Therapists)

Hawaii

Administrator
 (Certification)
 Office of Personnel Services
 State Department of Education
 P.O. Box 2360
 Honolulu 96804
 (808) 548-6384
 (School Counselors)

Idaho

State Department of Education
 Len B. Jordan Building
 650 West State Street
 Boise 83720
 (208) 334-3475
 (School Counselors)

Barry Watts, Chairperson
 Idaho State Counselor Licensure Board
 Board of Occupational Licensure
 2404 Bank Drive
 Room 312
 Boise 83705-2598
 (208) 334-3233
 (Counselors in Nonschool Settings)

Illinois

Illinois State Board of Education
 Department of Teacher Education and Certification
 100 North First Street
 Springfield 62777
 (217) 782-3774
 (School Counselors)

Illinois Certification Boards, Inc.
 28 West Madison
 Suite 201
 Oak Park 60302
 (312) 848-9445

Illinois Addiction Counselor Certification Board
 104 North 4th Street
 Springfield 62701
 (217) 544-4035
 (Both for Alcohol and Drug Abuse Counselors)

Indiana

Indiana Department of Education
 Teacher Certification
 Room 229, State House
 Indianapolis 46204-2798
 (317) 232-9010
 (School Counselors)

Indiana Counselor Association on
    Alcohol and Drug Abuse,
    Inc.
  1800 North Meridian Street
  Suite 507
  Indianapolis 46202
  (317) 923-8800
  (Alcohol and Drug Abuse
    Counselors)

Iowa

Division of Teacher Education and
    Certification
  Department of Education
  Grimes State Office Building
  Des Moines 50319-0146
  (515) 281-3245
(School Counselors)

Iowa Board of Substance Abuse
    Certification
  P.O. Box 7284
  Grand Avenue Station
  Des Moines 50309
  (515) 281-7039
  (Alcohol and Drug Abuse
    Counselors)

Kansas

Certification Section
  State Department of Education
  120 East 10th Street
  Topeka 66612
  (913) 296-2288
  (School Counselors)

Kansas Alcohol and Drug Abuse
    Counselors Association
  P.O. Box 1732
  Topeka 66601
  (913) 233-7145
  (Alcohol and Drug Abuse
    Counselors)

A board for counselors in non-school settings is to be established.

Kentucky

State Department of Education
  Division of Teacher Education
    and Certification
  18th Floor, CPT
  Frankfort 40601
  (502) 564-4606
  (School Counselors)

Kentucky Chemical Dependency
    Counselors' Professional Certification Board
  P.O. Box 21891
  Lexington 45022-1891
  (no phone)
  (Alcohol and Drug Abuse
    Counselors)

Louisiana

Bureau of Higher Education and
    Certification
  State Department of Education
  P.O. Box 94064
  Baton Rouge 70804
  (504) 342-3490
  (School Counselors)

Susan Smith, Secretary
  Licensed Professional Counselors
  Board of Examiners
  123 Peabody Hall
  Louisiana State University
  Baton Rouge 70503-4121
  (504) 388-2213
  (Counselors in Nonschool Settings)

Certification Examining Board of LASACT, Inc.
  P.O. Box 80235
  Baton Rouge 70898-0235
  (no phone)
  (Alcohol and Drug Abuse Counselors)

Maine

State Department of Education
  Division of Professional Services
  State House Station 23
  Augusta 04330
  (207) 289-5944
  (School Counselors)

Maryland

Certification Branch
  State Department of Education
  200 West Baltimore Street
  Baltimore 21201
  (301) 333-2142
  (School Counselors)

Aileen Taylor
  Maryland Board of Examiners of Professional Counselors
  201 West Preston Street
  Room 103
  Baltimore 21201
  (301) 225-5835
  (Counselors in Nonschool Settings)

Maryland Addictions Counselor Certification Board
  P.O. Box 3341
  Frederick 21701
  (301) 865-3021
  (Alcohol and Drug Abuse Counselors)

Massachusetts

Bureau of Teacher Preparation, Certification and Placement
  Commonwealth Department of Education
  1385 Hancock Street
  Quincy 02169
  (617) 770-7517
  (School Counselors)

The Massachusetts Committee for Voluntary Certification of Alcoholism Counselors, Inc.
  560 Lincoln Street
  P.O. Box 7070
  Worcester 01605
  (617) 752-8070
  (Alcohol and Drug Abuse Counselors)

Boards for counselors in nonschool settings and for marriage and family therapists are to be established.

Michigan

Michigan Department of Education
Division of Teacher Education and Certification
Teacher Education and Certification Services
P.O. Box 30008
Lansing 48909
(517) 373-1924
(School Counselors)

Marriage Counseling Board
Department of Licensing and Regulation
Box 30018
Lansing 48909
Attn: Sharon Pickens
(517) 373-1870/1653
(Marriage and Family Therapists)

Michigan Institute for Human Resource Development
B-304 Ellsworth Hall
Western Michigan University
Kalamazoo 49008
(616) 383-1536
(Alcohol and Drug Abuse Counselors)

A board for counselors in nonschool settings is to be established.

Minnesota

Certification Section
State Department of Education
616 Capitol Square Building
550 Cedar Street
Saint Paul 55101
(612) 296-2046
(School Counselors)

Board of Marriage and Family Therapy
Office of Social Work and Mental Health Boards
2700 University Avenue West, #225
St. Paul 55414
Attn: Deborah Mancheski, Exec. Director
(612) 643-2580
(Marriage and Family Therapists)

Institute for Chemical Dependency Professionals of Minnesota, Inc.
596 South Osceola Avenue
St. Paul 55102
(612) 227-7584
(Alcohol and Drug Abuse Counselors)

Mississippi

Office of Teacher Education
State Department of Education
P.O. Box 771
Jackson 39205
(601) 359-3483
(School Counselors)

Mississippi Association of Alcohol and Drug Abuse Counselors
P.O. Box 3507
Meridian 39303
(601) 693-0126
(Alcohol and Drug Abuse Counselors)

A board for counselors in nonschool settings is to be established.

Missouri

State Department of Education
Certification Office
P.O. Box 480
Jefferson City 65102
(314) 751-3486
(School Counselors)

Ms. Charlotte King
Division of Professional Registry
P.O. Box 153
Jefferson City 65102
(314) 751-2334, ext. 200
(Counselors in Nonschool Settings)

Missouri Substance Abuse Counselor Certification Board
P.O. Box 1673
Columbia 65205
(314) 443-5521
(Alcohol and Drug Abuse Counselors)

Montana

Office of Public Instruction
Certification Department
State Capitol, Room 106
Helena 59620
(406) 444-3150
(School Counselors)

Mary Hainlin
Board of Social Work Examiners and Licensed Professional Counselors
1424 9th Avenue
Helena 59620
(406) 444-4285
(Counselors in Nonschool Settings)

Nebraska

Nebraska Department of Education
Teacher Education and Certification Office
301 Centennial Mall South
P.O. Box 94987
Lincoln 68509
(402) 471-2496
(School Counselors)

Kris Chiles
Associate Director
Bureau of Examining Boards
Centennial Mall South
P.O. Box 95007
Lincoln 68509-5007
(402) 471-2115
(Counselors in Nonschool Settings)

Nevada

Department of Education
  Teacher Certification Office
  400 West King Street
  Carson City 89710
  (702) 885-3115
  (School Counselors)

Board of Marriage and Family
  Therapist Examiners
  1455 East Tropicana Avenue,
    Suite 470
  Las Vegas 89119
  Attn: Mary Forrester
  (702) 486-7188
  (Marriage and Family
    Therapists)

New Hampshire

Department of Education
  Bureau of Certification
  101 Pleasant Street
  Concord 03301
  (603) 271-2407
  (School Counselors)

New Hampshire Office of Alcohol
    and Substance Abuse Prevention
  6 Hazen Drive
  Concord 03301
  (603) 271-4625
  (Alcohol and Drug Abuse
    Counselors)

New Jersey

New Jersey Department of Education
  Office of Teacher Certification
    and Academic Credentials
  3535 Quaker Bridge Road
  CN-503
  Trenton 08625-0503
  (609) 588-3100
  (Student Personnel Services)

Board of Marriage Counselor Examiners
  1100 Raymond Blvd., Rm. 512
  Newark 07012
  Attn: Jeanette Balber
  (201) 648-2534
  (Marriage and Family
    Therapists)

New Jersey Alcoholism Counselor
    Certification Board
  90 Monmouth Street
  Suite 202
  Red Bank 07701
  (201) 741-3835
  (Alcohol Abuse Counselors)

New Jersey Substance Abuse
    Counselor Certification
    Board
  90 Monmouth Street
  Suite 202
  Red Bank 07701
  (201) 758-9047
  (Drug Abuse Counselors)

New Mexico

Department of Education
 Teacher Licensing Unit
 Education Building
 Santa Fe 87503
 (505) 827-6587
 (School Counselors)

New Mexico Alcohol and Drug
  Abuse Counselor Association
 Certification Board
 7711 Zuni Road, SE
 Albuquerque 87108
 (505) 265-6811
 (Alcohol and Drug Abuse
  Counselors)

New York

New York State Department of
  Education
 Division of Teacher Certification
 Cultural Education Center
 Madison Avenue
 Rm 5A-11
 Albany 12230
 (518) 474-3901
 (School Counselors)

North Carolina

State Department of Public Instruction
 Division of Certification
 116 West Edenton Street
 Raleigh 27603-1712
 (919) 733-4125
 (School Counselors)

Marital and Family Therapy Certification Board
 Section on Marriage and Family Therapy
 Department of Psychiatry
 Bowman Gray School of
  Medicine
 Winston-Salem 27103
 Attn: Sheila Beck, Executive
  Secretary
 (919) 748-4657
 (Marriage and Family
  Therapists)

Dr. Don C. Locke
 Chairperson
 North Carolina Registered Practicing Counselors
 Box 19264
 Raleigh 27619
 (919) 737-2244
 (Counselors in General)

North Dakota

Department of Public Instruction
 Teacher Certification
 Capitol Building
 600 East Boulevard Avenue
 Bismarck 58505
 (701) 224-2264
 (School Counselors)

Ohio

State Department of Education
Teacher Certification
65 South Front Street
Room 1012
Columbus 43266-0308
(614) 466-3593
(School Counselors)

Beth Farnsworth, Executive Secretary
State of Ohio Counselor and Social Worker Board
77 South High Street
16th Floor
Columbus 43266
(614) 466-6463
(Counselors in Nonschool Settings)

Ohio Chemical Dependency Counselors Credentialing Board, Inc.
274 Marconi Boulevard
Suite 420
Columbus 43215
(614) 461-4035
(Alcohol and Drug Abuse Counselors)

Oklahoma

State Department of Education
Department of Teacher Education and Certification
2500 North Lincoln Boulevard
Oklahoma City 73105
(405) 521-3337
(School Counselors)

Dr. Mike Blazi, Administrator
Licensed Professional Counselors Committee
1000 NE 10th Street
Oklahoma City 73152
(405) 271-6030
(Counselors in Nonschool Settings)

Oklahoma Association on Alcohol and Other Drug Abuse Counselor Certification Board
2248 North Moore Avenue
Moore 73160
(405) 793-1545
(Alcohol and Drug Abuse Counselors)

Oregon

Teacher Standards and Practices Commission
630 Center Street, NE
Suite 200
Salem 97310
(503) 378-3586
(School Counselors)

Pennsylvania

Commonwealth Department of Education
Bureau of Teacher Preparation and Certification
333 Market Street
Harrisburg 17126-0333
(717) 787-2968
(School Counselors)

Pennsylvania Certified Addiction
 Counselors Board
4751 Lindle Road
Suite 113, Host Inn
Harrisburg 17111-9986
(717) 939-2950
(Alcohol and Drug Abuse
 Counselors)

Rhode Island

State Department of Education
 Teacher Certification
 22 Hayes Street
 Providence 02908
 (401) 277-2675
 (School Counselors)

Concetta DaSilva
 Department of Health,
 Division of Professional
 Regulation
 75 Davis Street
 Cannon Building, Room 104
 Providence 02908
 (401) 277-2827
 (Counselors in Nonschool Settings and Marriage and Family Therapists)

South Carolina

State Department of Education
 Teacher Certification Department
 1015 Rutledge Building
 Columbia 29201
 (803) 734-8466
 (School Counselors)

Ms. Jan Simpson
 Administrative Secretary
 Board of Examiners for Counselors and Therapists
 P.O. Box 7965
 Columbia 29202
 (803) 734-1765
 (Counselors in Nonschool Settings and Marriage and Family Therapists)

South Dakota

South Dakota Department of Education and Cultural Affairs
 Division of Teacher Education and Certification
 Pierre 57501
 (605) 773-3553
 (School Counselors)

South Dakota Chemical Dependency Counselors Certification Board
 P.O. Box 102
 Yankton 57078
 (605) 665-1028
 (Alcohol and Drug Abuse
  Counselors)

Tennessee

Department of Education
 Office of Teacher Licenses
 125 Cordell Hull Building
 Nashville 37219-5338
 (615) 741-1644
 (School Counselors)

Buster Walker
  Tennessee State Board of
    Professional Counselors and
    Marital & Family Therapists
  283 Plus Park Blvd.
  Nashville 37219-5407
  (615) 367-6207
  (Counselors in Nonschool Settings and Marriage and Family Therapists)

Texas

Texas Department of Education
  Division of Teacher Education
    and Certification
  201 East 11th Street
  Austin 78701
  (512) 463-8976
  (School Counselors)

Mr. Daniel Boone
  Texas Board of Examiners for
    Professional Counselors
  1100 West 49th Street
  Austin 78756
  (512) 458-7111
  (Counselors in Nonschool Settings)

Texas Certification Board for Alcohol and Drug Abuse Counselors
  5510 IH North
  Austin 78751
  (512) 459-3305
  (Alcohol and Drug Abuse Counselors)

Utah

State Office of Education
  Teacher Certification
  250 East 500 South
  Salt Lake City 84111
  (801) 538-7740
  (School Counselors)

Division of Occupational and
    Professional Licensing
  Department of Business Regulations
  Heber M. Wells Building
  160 East 300 South
  P.O. Box 45802
  Salt Lake City 84145
  (801) 530-6633 or 530-6628
  (Marriage and Family Therapists)

Utah Association of Alcohol and
    Drug Abuse Counselors
  P.O. Box 26332
  Salt Lake City 84126
  (Alcohol and Drug Abuse Counselors)

Vermont

Department of Education
  Teacher Certification
  120 State Street
  Montpelier 05602
  (802) 828-2445
  (School Counselors)

Nancy Weber
 270 College Street
 Burlington 05401
 (802) 862-3101
 (Counselors in Nonschool Settings)

Vermont Alcoholism and Drug Abuse Counselor Association
 P.O. Box 562
 Newport 05855
 (802) 334-8634
 (Alcohol and Drug Abuse Counselors)

Virginia

State Department of Education
 Teacher Certification
 Box 6Q
 Richmond 23216
 (804) 225-2022
 (School Counselors)

Stephanie Sivert
 Department of Health Regulatory Boards
 Virginia Board of Professional Counselors
 1601 Rolling Hills Drive
 2d Floor
 Richmond 23229-5005
 (804) 662-9912
 (Counselors in Nonschool Settings)

Washington

Professional Certification
 Old Capitol Building
 FG-11
 Olympia 98504
 (206) 753-6773
 (School Counselors)

Theresa Fitzgerald
 Licensing Coordinator
 Department of Licensing
 Division of Professional Licensing
 P.O. Box 9649
 Olympia 98504
 (206) 753-6936
 (Counselors in Nonschool Settings and Marriage and Family Therapists)

West Virginia

West Virginia Department of Education
 Certification Unit
 Capitol Complex
 Building 6, Room B-337
 Charleston 25305
 (304) 348-2703
 (School Counselors)

Charles Maine, Secretary
 West Virginia Board of Examiners in Counseling
 P.O. Box 6492
 Charleston 25362
 (304) 345-3852
 (Counselors in Nonschool Settings)

West Virginia Alcoholism and
Drug Abuse Counselor Certification Board
P.O. Box 1257
Morgantown 26507
(304) 292-6046
(Alcohol and Drug Abuse
Counselors)

Wisconsin

Department of Public Instruction
Certification Section
125 South Webster Street
P.O. Box 7841
Madison 53707
(608) 266-1027
(School Counselors)

Wisconsin Alcoholism and Drug
Abuse Counselor Certification Board, Inc.
416 East Main Street
Waukesha 53186
(414) 542-4144

Wyoming

State Department of Education
Certification Licensing Unit
Hathaway Building
Cheyenne 82002
(307) 777-7291
(School Counselors)

Dr. Helene Graves, Chair
Professional Counselors, Marriage and Family Therapists,
Social Workers, and Chemical Dependency Specialists
Licensure Board
P.O. Box 591
Cheyenne 82003
(307) 635-2817
(Counselors in Nonschool
Settings and Marriage and
Family Therapists)